OUR BEST
200+
HOLiDAY
QUiCKiES

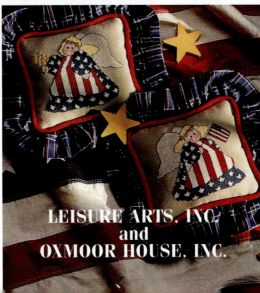

LEISURE ARTS, INC.
and
OXMOOR HOUSE, INC.

EDITORIAL STAFF

Vice President and Editor-in-Chief:
   Anne Van Wagner Childs
Executive Director: Sandra Graham Case
Editorial Director: Susan Frantz Wiles
Publications Director: Carla Bentley
Creative Art Director: Gloria Bearden
Senior Graphics Art Director: Melinda Stout

EDITORIAL
Managing Editor: Linda L. Trimble
Associate Editor: Darla Burdette Kelsay
Assistant Editors: Tammi Williamson Bradley,
   Terri Leming Davidson, and Robyn Sheffield-Edwards
Copy Editor: Laura Lee Weland

TECHNICAL
Senior Publications Editor: Sherry Taylor O'Connor
Managing Editor: Lisa Truxton Curton
Special Projects Editor: Connie White Irby
Senior Production Assistant: Martha H. Carle
Production Assistants: Andrea Ahlen, Mary Hutcheson,
   Lisa Hinkle Lancaster, and Jennifer S. Potts

ART
Book/Magazine Graphics Art Director:
   Diane M. Hugo
Graphics Illustrator: Guniz Jernigan
Photography Stylists: Sondra Daniel, Laura Dell,
   Aurora Huston, and Courtney Jones

BUSINESS STAFF
Publisher: Bruce Akin
Vice President, Marketing: Guy A. Crossley
Marketing Manager: Byron L. Taylor
Print Production Manager: Laura Lockhart
Vice President and General Manager: Thomas L. Carlisle
Retail Sales Director: Richard Tignor
Vice President, Retail Marketing: Pam Stebbins
Retail Marketing Director: Margaret Sweetin
Retail Customer Services Manager: Carolyn Pruss
General Merchandise Manager: Russ Barnett
Vice President, Finance: Tom Siebenmorgen
Distribution Director: Ed M. Strackbein

Library of Congress Catalog Number 97-70453
Hardcover ISBN 0-8487-4157-9
Softcover ISBN 1-57486-061-5

OUR BEST

200+ HOLIDAY QUICKIES

Cross stitching is one of our favorite ways to prepare for holidays, whether we're making decorations for our homes or creating fabulous gifts. The cross stitcher's dream book, Our Best 200+ Holiday Quickies offers an invaluable assortment of fast-to-finish projects for occasions from Valentine's Day to Christmas. There are oodles of designs to frame, as well as embellishments for clothing and other accessories. You'll also find plenty of motifs for linens, bookmarks, mugs, jar lids, ornaments, totes, and more. With this one-stop volume of fun, celebrating holidays will be easier than ever!

TABLE OF CONTENTS

VALENTiNE'S DAY

Valentine's Day offers the perfect opportunity to shower those dear to you with little tokens of affection. This heartwarming collection includes an array of romantic and thoughtful gifts such as these Love Bears. The decorative pillow reminds us that hearts are always in need of love! You'll also find a sentimental picture frame for displaying a photo of your sweetheart, a collection of forget-me-not mugs, and more.

Design by Kathie Rueger.
Needlework adaptation by
Marilyn Vestring.

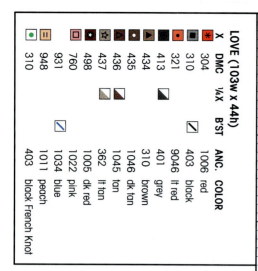

X	¼X	B'ST	DMC	ANC.	COLOR
			304	1006	red
			310	403	black
			321	9046	lt red
			413	401	grey
			434	310	brown
			435	1046	dk tan
			436	1045	tan
			437	362	lt tan
			498	1005	dk red
			760	1022	pink
			931	1034	blue
			948	1011	peach
			310	403	black French Knot

The design was stitched on a 16" x 12" piece of Ivory Aida (14 ct). Three strands of floss were used for Cross Stitch and 1 strand for Backstitch and French Knots. It was made into a pillow.

PILLOW FINISHING

Note: Use a ½" seam allowance for all seams.

Trim stitched piece to 13" x 8". Cut a piece of backing fabric the same size.

For cording, center a 45" length of ³⁄₈" dia. cord on wrong side of a 2" x 45" bias fabric strip. Matching edges, fold strip over cord. Using zipper foot, baste close to cord; trim seam allowances to ½". Matching raw edges, pin cording to right side of stitched piece, making a ³⁄₈" clip in seam allowances of cording at each corner. Pin overlapping end of cording out of the way. Starting 1½" from beginning of cording and ending 3" from overlapping end, sew cording to stitched piece. On overlapping end, remove 2" of basting; fold end of fabric back and trim cord so it meets beginning end of cord. Fold end of fabric under ½"; wrap fabric over beginning end of cording. Finish sewing cording to stitched piece.

For ruffle, press short ends of a 6" x 105" piece of fabric ½" to wrong side. Matching wrong sides, fold fabric in half lengthwise. Gather raw edge of ruffle to fit stitched piece. Matching raw edges, pin ruffle to right side of stitched piece; sew ruffle to stitched piece. Join ends of ruffle using blind stitches.

Matching right sides and leaving an opening for turning, sew stitched piece and backing fabric together. Trim corners diagonally. Turn pillow right side out. Stuff pillow with polyester fiberfill; sew final closure by hand. Refer to photo to attach button and jute bow to pillow.

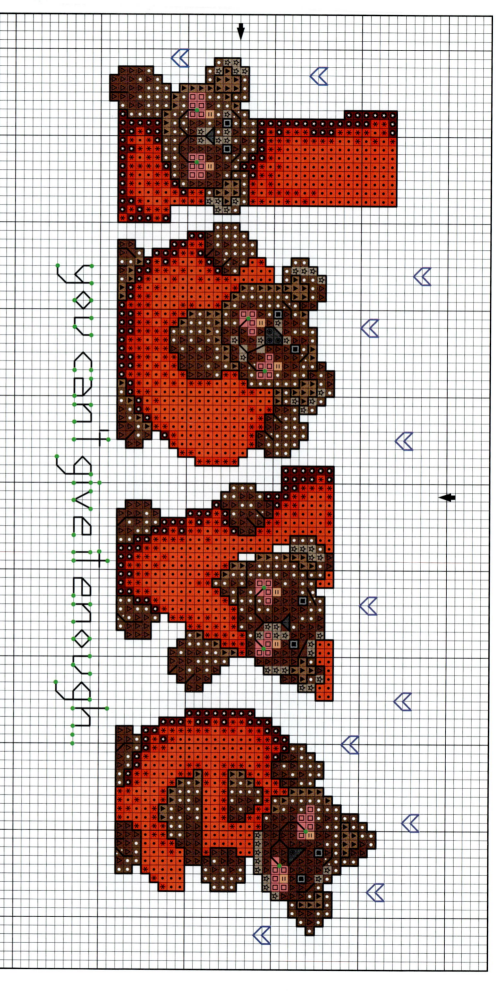

FROM THE HEART

Trimmed with tiny hearts and lining a basketful of tasty treats, this dainty bread cover will make a sentimental gift for someone sweet.

VALENTINE BREAD COVER (66w x 66h)

X	DMC	¼X	B'ST	ANC.	COLOR
✔	666		✓	46	red
Π	892	◢		33	pink
▽	894			27	lt pink
	909		✓	923	green
✖	911			205	lt green

The design was stitched in one corner of a white bread cover (14 ct), 6 squares from beginning of fringe on each side. Three strands of floss were used for Cross Stitch and 1 strand for Backstitch.

Design by Kathy Werkmeister.

9

If your cup runneth over with love, make sure your special someone knows about it. These forget-me-not mugs will deliver your valentine message with warmth.

Each design was stitched on a 10¼" x 3½" piece of Vinyl-Weave® (14 ct). For **Design #1**, 2 strands of floss were used for all stitches. For **Designs #2** and **#3**, 3 strands of floss were used for Cross Stitch and 1 for all other stitches. For design placement, center mug design on right half of vinyl if mug is for a right-handed person or on left half of vinyl if mug is for a left-handed person. Each design was inserted in a red mug. Hand wash mug to protect stitchery.

Designs by Sam Hawkins.

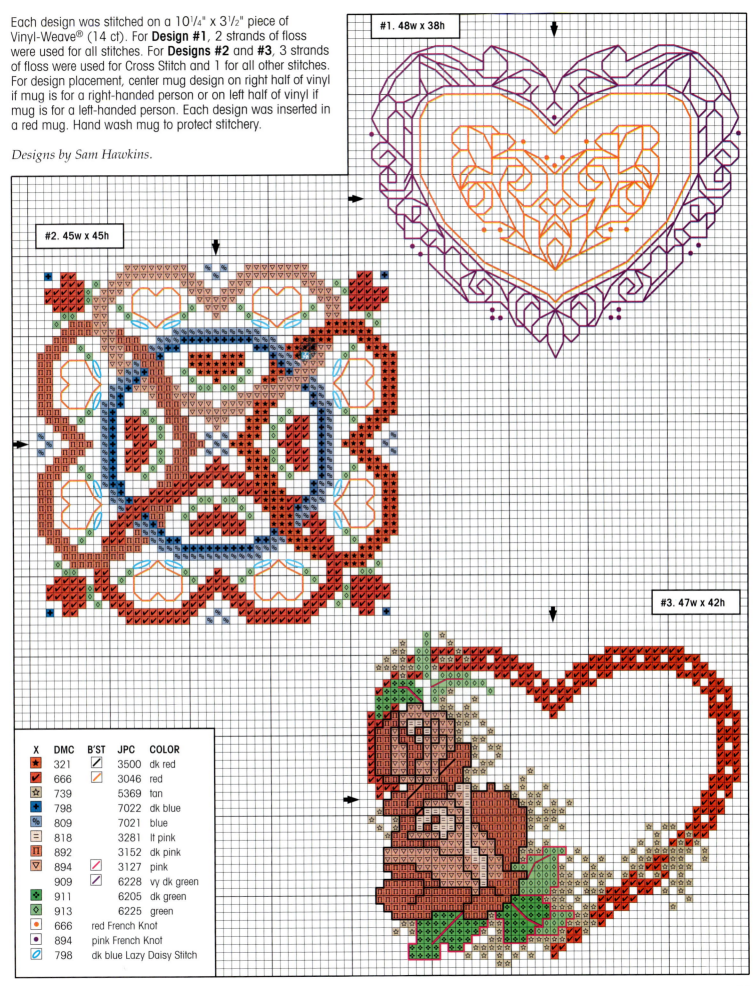

#1. 48w x 38h

#2. 45w x 45h

#3. 47w x 42h

X	DMC	B'ST	JPC	COLOR
★	321	◢	3500	dk red
✔	666	◿	3046	red
☆	739		5369	tan
✚	798		7022	dk blue
%	809		7021	blue
=	818		3281	lt pink
Π	892		3152	dk pink
▽	894	◢	3127	pink
	909	◢	6228	vy dk green
◈	911		6205	dk green
◇	913		6225	green
●	666			red French Knot
●	894			pink French Knot
◐	798			dk blue Lazy Daisy Stitch

11

VICTORIAN VALENTINE FRAME

Pretty pearl seed beads and delicate stitches lend a Victorian air to this picture frame. It'll make a wonderful present for a loving couple, especially with their photograph tucked inside.

57w x 71h

	X	DMC	B'ST	LONG STITCH	ANC.
		ecru			387

00123 cream Mill Hill Seed Beads

Pink lines indicate outside and inside cutting line.

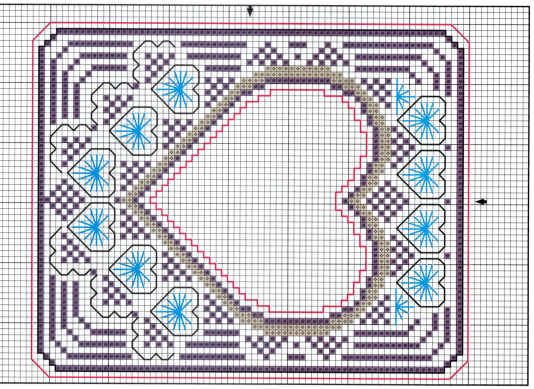

The design was stitched on a 9" x 10" piece of Brown perforated paper (14 ct). Two strands of floss were used for all stitches. It was made into a photo frame; see Photo Frame Finishing, page 143.

Design by Kathy Elrod.

BE MINE!

Dainty flowers and a loving plea take center stage on our dreamy pillow. Finished with a lace ruffle, satin ribbons, and golden charms, it'll make an enchanting gift for the romantic at heart.

64w x 47h

X	DMC	B'ST	COLOR
•	blanc		white
■	310		black
★	321		red
▼	333		dk purple
✳	340		purple
	535	╱	grey
◆	561		dk blue green
◆	562		blue green
⬠	699		green
‖	702		yellow green
♡	704		lt yellow green
○	740		orange
◣	742		yellow
⊙	956		dk pink
☐	957		pink
+	3753		lt blue

The design was stitched over 2 fabric threads on an 11" x 10" piece of White Irish Linen (28 ct). Three strands of floss were used for Cross Stitch and 1 for Backstitch. It was made into a pillow; see Be Mine Pillow Finishing, page 143.

Design by Barbara Baatz, Kooler Design Studio.

With a knowing smile, this little candy-store clerk tells us that "nothing's sweeter than love." What a heartwarming thought to share on Valentine's Day!

NOTHING'S SWEETER (54w x 54h)

X	DMC	¼X	B'ST	JPC	COLOR
•	blanc	◩		1001	white
ø	209			4302	violet
	310		◩	8403	black
4	318	◩		8511	grey
✖	320	◩		6017	green
E	347	◩	◩	3013	red
U	368	◩		6016	lt green
♥	434			5000	dk tan
T	435	◩		5371	tan
X	437	◩		5942	lt tan
>	725			2294	gold
P	754	◩		2331	peach
5	760			3069	rose
2	762	◩		8510	lt grey
✦	930	◩		7052	blue
•·	310				black French Knot

The design was stitched on a 9" square of Ivory Aida (14 ct). Two strands of floss were used for Cross Stitch and 1 for all other stitches. It was inserted in a 5" square frame.

Design by Sisters Two, Inc.

CUPID BEAR

Stitched on a sweatshirt, this whimsical bear will inspire you to play Cupid. His romantic spirit is sure to be contagious!

CUPID BEAR (59w x 51h)

X	DMC	¼X	B'ST	COLOR
•	blanc			white
■	310	◩	⁄	black
★	321			lt red
4	415			lt grey
■	433			brown
♥	434			lt brown
T	435	◩		vy lt brown
•	436			dk tan
×	437	◩		tan
\	738	◩		lt tan
2	762			vy lt grey
•	310	black French Knot		

The design was stitched over an 11" x 10" piece of 8.5 mesh waste canvas on a white sweatshirt. Six strands of floss were used for Cross Stitch and 2 strands for Backstitch and French Knots. See Working on Waste Canvas, page 143.

Design by Kathie Rueger.

Inspired by French country and Victorian-style fabrics, these fanciful towels are the essence of l'amour. They'll make lovely tokens of your affection, or you can hang them in your bath for an air of elegance.

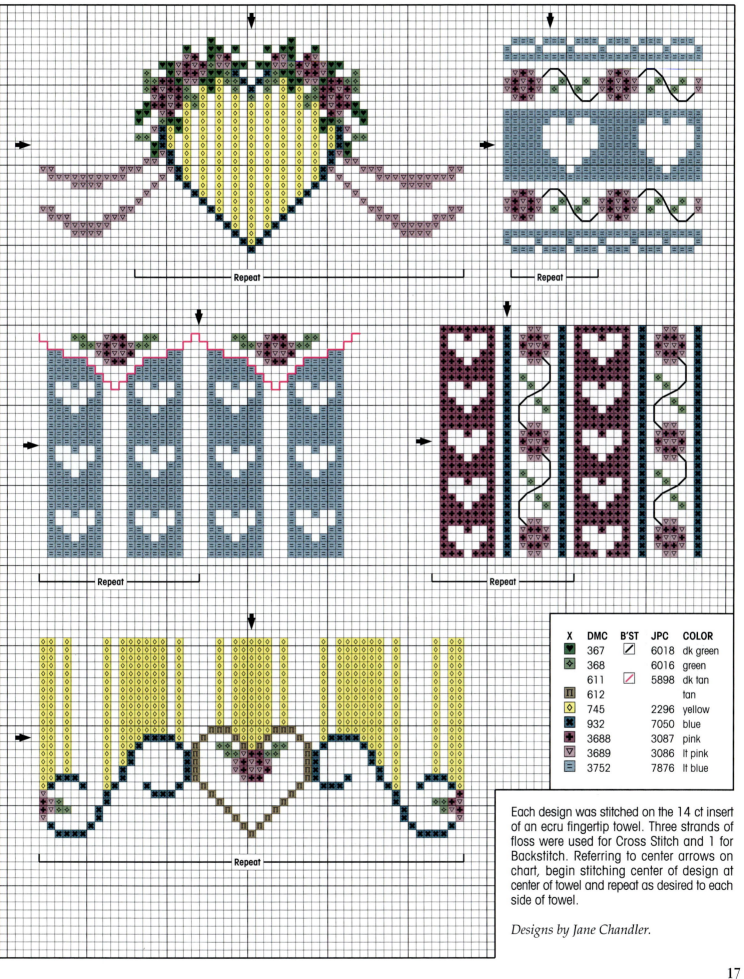

X	DMC	B'ST	JPC	COLOR
▼	367	/	6018	dk green
✦	368		6016	green
	611	/	5898	dk tan
⊓	612			tan
◇	745		2296	yellow
✖	932		7050	blue
✚	3688		3087	pink
▽	3689		3086	lt pink
☰	3752		7876	lt blue

Each design was stitched on the 14 ct insert of an ecru fingertip towel. Three strands of floss were used for Cross Stitch and 1 for Backstitch. Referring to center arrows on chart, begin stitching center of design at center of towel and repeat as desired to each side of towel.

Designs by Jane Chandler.

17

ST. PATRiCK'S DAY

Since the early 1700's when Irish immigrants introduced us to the fun-filled occasion, Americans have celebrated St. Patrick's Day in honor of the patron saint of Ireland. Today we continue the tradition by tucking shamrocks in our lapels and wearing green clothing. This collection pays homage to the Emerald Isle and its great people with several Irish blessings, such as the one shown here, along with a shirt, a wreath, and a cute mug for the "beary" Irish!

May your neighbors
respect you,
Trouble neglect you,
The angels protect you,
And Heaven
accent you.

-Author Unknown

May your neighbors respect you,
Trouble neglect you,
The angels protect you,
And heaven accent you.

—Author Unknown—

The design was stitched over two fabric threads on a 13½" x 12" piece of Cream Lugana (25 ct). Three strands of floss were used for Cross Stitch and 1 for Backstitch and French Knots. It was custom framed.

Design by Terrie Lee Steinmeyer.

AN IRISH BLESSING (90w x 75h)

X	DMC	¼X	B'ST	ANC.	COLOR	X	DMC	¼X	B'ST	ANC.	COLOR
•	blanc	◿		2	white	✔	987			244	green
‖	744			301	yellow	•	988			243	lt green
	895		╱	1044	vy dk green	═	989	◿	╱	242	vy lt green
T	927		╱	848	lt grey	•	895				vy dk green French Knot
✔	986		╱	246	dk green						

A sweatshirt with this traditional Irish design will bring good luck to anyone who wears it — and that's no blarney!

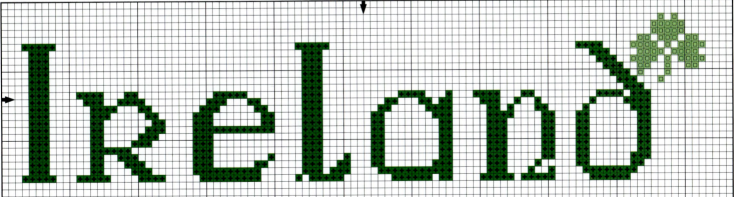

IRELAND (100w x 24h)

X	DMC	JPC	COLOR
✚	909	6228	green
☐	911	6205	lt green

The design was stitched over a 14" x 6" piece of 10 mesh waste canvas on a white sweatshirt. Five strands of floss were used for Cross Stitch. See Working on Waste Canvas, page 143.

Design by Denise Cagney.

Planning a St. Patrick's Day gathering? Hang this whimsical welcome on your door to ensure that all your visitors are dressed appropriately — in green!

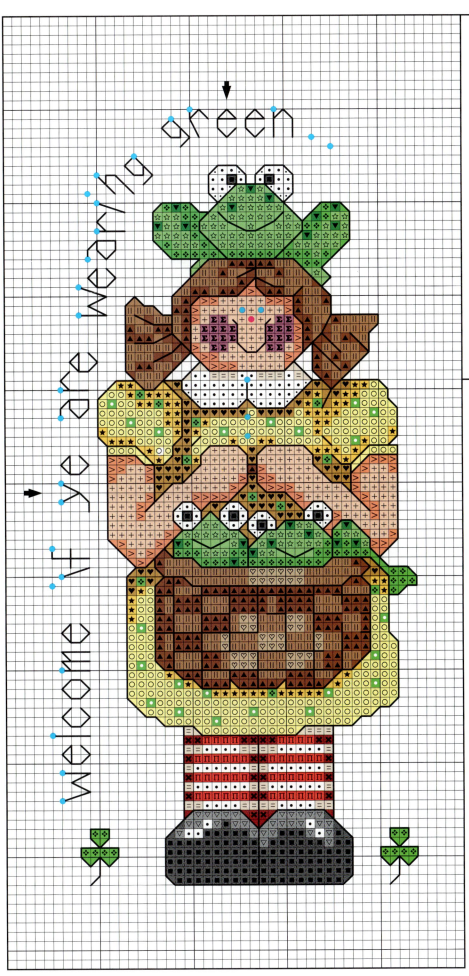

X	DMC	1/4X	B'ST	ANC.	COLOR
				WELCOME IF YE ARE WEARING GREEN (40w x 84h)	
•	blanc			2	white
=	ecru			387	ecru
✖	304			1006	red
■	310		╱	403	black
▽	317			400	grey
∏	321			9046	lt red
‖	420			374	brown
♡	422			373	lt brown
★	725			305	yellow
○	726			295	lt yellow
+	754			1012	flesh
>	758			882	dk flesh
▼	783			307	gold
▲	869			944	dk brown
▼	895			1044	vy dk green
✦	904			258	dk green
•	905			257	green
☆	906			256	lt green
Σ	3326			36	pink
●	310				black French Knot
●	321				lt red French Knot

The design was stitched on an 11" x 14" piece of Antique White Aida (14 ct). Three strands of floss were used for Cross Stitch and 1 strand for Backstitch and French Knots. It was inserted in a purchased frame (5" x 7" opening) and attached to a decorated grapevine wreath.

Design by Kathie Rueger.
Needlework adaptation by Jane Chandler and Christine Street.

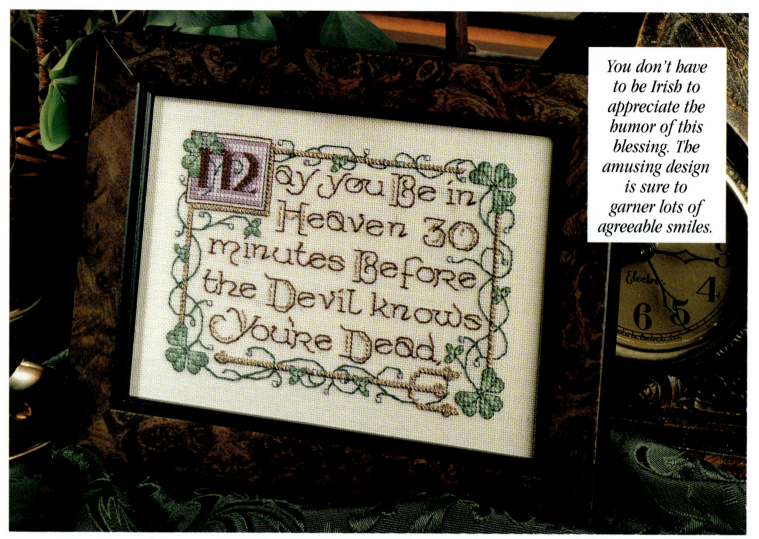

You don't have to be Irish to appreciate the humor of this blessing. The amusing design is sure to garner lots of agreeable smiles.

X	DMC	¼X	B'ST	COLOR
🟣	209			purple
💜	211			lt purple
	561		✏	dk green
	561		✏ *	dk green
💚	562			green
⬛	898		✏	brown
	898		✏ *	brown
➕	954			lt green
☆ †			✏ †	gold metallic

* Use 2 strands of floss.
† Use 1 strand of Kreinik Fine (#8) Braid - 221.

The design was stitched over two fabric threads on a 10" x 8" piece of Cream Belfast Linen (32 ct). Two strands of floss were used for Cross Stitch and 1 strand for Backstitch (unless otherwise indicated in color key). It was inserted in a purchased frame (7" x 5" opening).

Design by Sandy Orton, Kooler Design Studio.

84w x 57h

"BEARY" IRISH MUG

This "beary" Irish leprechaun mug is just right for serving up hot Irish coffee.

"BEARY" IRISH MUG (52w x 45h)

X	DMC	B'ST	JPC	COLOR
•	blanc		1001	white
■	310	✓	8403	black
▽	317		8512	grey
◉	434		5000	brown
◆	435		5371	dk tan
□	436		5943	tan
∗	437		5942	lt tan
★	725		2298	dk yellow
O	726		2295	yellow
⬊	727		2289	lt yellow
✚	909		6228	dk green
◉	910		6031	green
□	911		6205	lt green
✕	3072		6005	lt grey
▨	3799		8999	dk grey
•	310			black French Knot

The design was stitched on a 10¼" x 3½" piece of Vinyl-Weave® (14 ct). Three strands of floss were used for Cross Stitch, 1 for Backstitch, and 2 for French Knots. For design placement, center mug design on right half of vinyl if mug is for a right-handed person or on left half of vinyl if mug is for a left-handed person. The design was inserted in a green mug. Hand wash mug to protect stitchery.

Design by Kathie Rueger.
Needlework adaptation by Jane Chandler.

This gentle Irish blessing reminds us of the simple comforts and joys to be found in everyday life. It's especially nice for the holiday, but you'll want to display the touching message all year long.

Wishing you always—
Walls for the wind,
A roof for the rain,
Tea beside the fire,
Laughter to cheer you,
Those you love near you
And all that your heart
might desire.

Wishing you always—
Walls for the wind,
A roof for the rain,
Tea beside the fire,
Laughter to cheer you,
Those you love near you,
And all that your heart
might desire.

GENTLE BLESSING (65w x 80h)

X	DMC	B'ST	JPC	COLOR
◇	890	∕	6021	green
•	890			green French Knot

The design was stitched over two fabric threads on a 13" x 14" piece of Tea-Dyed Irish Linen (28 ct). Two strands of floss were used for all stitches. It was custom framed.

Design by Denise Cagney.

EASTER

Green grass and warm sunshine push aside the ice and snow of winter, heralding the beginning of spring and the promise of Easter. The celebration of Christ's resurrection is cause for great rejoicing with sunrise services, chocolate bunnies, and hunts for colorful Easter eggs. It's also time for honoring loved ones with little gifts, such as these bookmarks. You'll find a basketful of Easter-inspired projects here for making your festivities "egg-stra" special!

BOOKMARKS (24w x 84h)

X	¼X	B'ST	DMC	ANC.	COLOR
•			blanc	2	white
+			221	897	vy dk rose
▷			223	895	dk rose
✕			224	893	rose
◐			225	1026	lt rose

X	¼X	B'ST	DMC	ANC.	COLOR
			520	862	dk green
O			522	860	green
◈			524	858	lt green
◉			676	891	gold
◣			677	886	lt gold

X	¼X	¾X	B'ST	DMC	ANC.	COLOR
◣				729	890	dk gold
✳				775	128	lt blue
✦				839	360	brown
□				840	379	lt brown
S				927	848	grey blue

X	B'ST	DMC	ANC.	COLOR
◨		930	1035	dk blue
◲		3325	129	blue
•		930		dk blue French Knot
✦		520		dk green Lazy Daisy
		522		green Lazy Daisy

The designs were stitched on prefinished ecru Stitch-n-Mark™ (18 ct) bookmarks. Two strands of floss were used for Cross Stitch and 1 for all other stitches. The ribbon trim was removed from two of the bookmarks.

Designs by Terrie Lee Steinmeyer.

COTTONTAIL COVER

"Anybunny" would love this bread cover with its cute little cottontails and brightly colored carrots, especially if it's wrapped around homemade goodies from you!

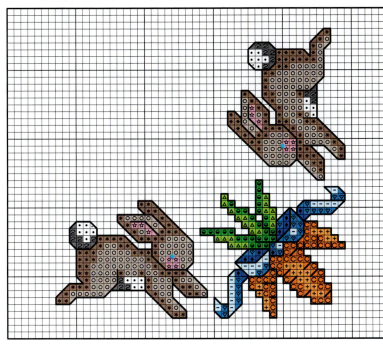

COTTONTAIL COVER (42w x 42h)

X	DMC	1/4X	COLOR	X	DMC	1/4X	B'ST	COLOR
•	blanc	◿	white	♥	813	◿		blue
◉	320		green	◆	826	◿		dk blue
△	368		lt green	−	827			lt blue
✳	437	◿	tan		938		◿	brown
◎	739	◿	lt tan	C	3340	◿		orange
☆	761	◿	pink	✚	3341			lt orange
2	762	◿	grey	•	938			brown French Knot

The design was stitched in one corner of a white bread cover (14 ct), 7 squares from beginning of fringe on each side. Three strands of floss were used for Cross Stitch and 1 strand for all other stitches.

Design by Lorraine Birmingham.

CHEERY TOPS

These bunny and chick designs are as cheery as spring, and they're quick to make, too! Just right for topping jars of candy or other treats, they also look precious on children's clothing.

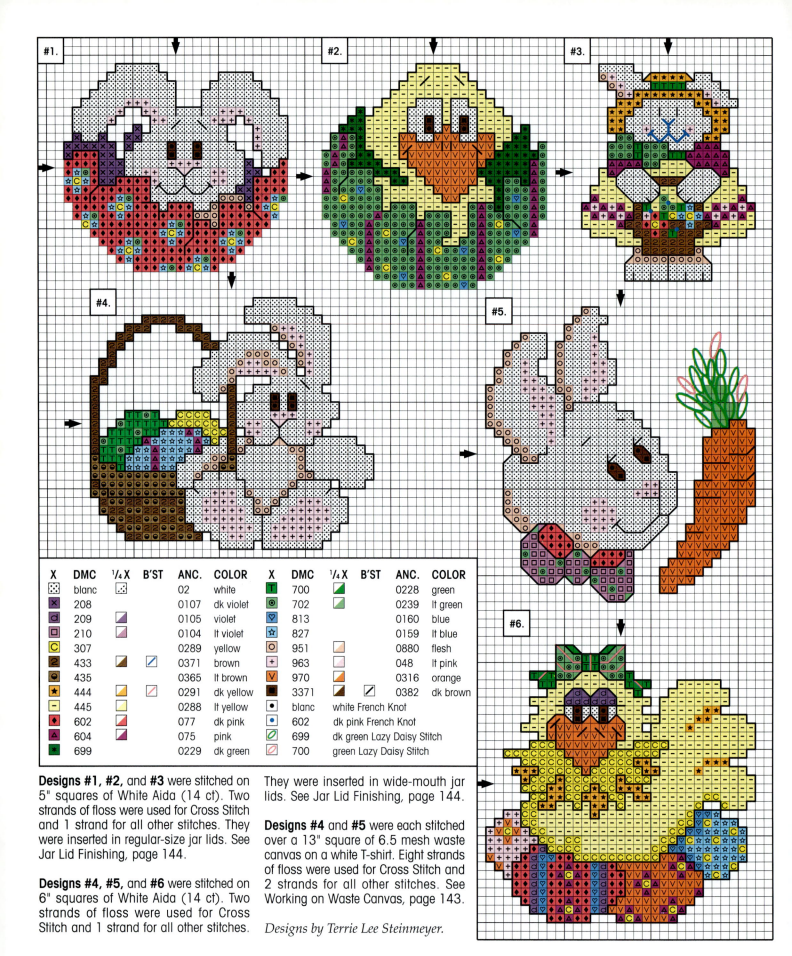

X	DMC	¼ X	B'ST	ANC.	COLOR	X	DMC	¼ X	B'ST	ANC.	COLOR
⊠	blanc	⊡		02	white	T	700	◤		0228	green
✕	208			0107	dk violet	◉	702	◤		0239	lt green
◩	209	◤		0105	violet	▽	813			0160	blue
▣	210			0104	lt violet	✭	827			0159	lt blue
C	307			0289	yellow	○	951			0880	flesh
2	433	◤	╱	0371	brown	+	963	◤		048	lt pink
◉	435			0365	lt brown	V	970			0316	orange
★	444	◤	╱	0291	dk yellow	◼	3371		╱	0382	dk brown
–	445	◤		0288	lt yellow	•	blanc			white French Knot	
◆	602	◤		077	dk pink	•	602			dk pink French Knot	
△	604	◤		075	pink	◢	699			dk green Lazy Daisy Stitch	
✱	699			0229	dk green	◢	700			green Lazy Daisy Stitch	

Designs #1, #2, and **#3** were stitched on 5" squares of White Aida (14 ct). Two strands of floss were used for Cross Stitch and 1 strand for all other stitches. They were inserted in regular-size jar lids. See Jar Lid Finishing, page 144.

Designs #4, #5, and **#6** were stitched on 6" squares of White Aida (14 ct). Two strands of floss were used for Cross Stitch and 1 strand for all other stitches.

They were inserted in wide-mouth jar lids. See Jar Lid Finishing, page 144.

Designs #4 and **#5** were each stitched over a 13" square of 6.5 mesh waste canvas on a white T-shirt. Eight strands of floss were used for Cross Stitch and 2 strands for all other stitches. See Working on Waste Canvas, page 143.

Designs by Terrie Lee Steinmeyer.

A "BEARY" FUNNY BUNNY

Sporting a whimsical floppy-eared cap, this playful bear poses as the Easter bunny! The "beary" funny bunny looks adorable stitched on a sweatshirt.

A "BEARY" FUNNY BUNNY (57w x 69h)

X	DMC	¼X	B'ST	JPC	COLOR
•	blanc			1001	white
■	310		✓	8403	black
▲	312			7979	blue
◆	322			7978	lt blue
⊙	336			7981	vy dk blue
V	415			8398	lt grey
	433			5471	brown
★	434			5000	lt brown
	435			5371	vy lt brown
⊡	436			5943	dk tan
▣	437			5942	tan
▣	702			6239	vy lt green
⊙	726			2295	lt yellow
	738			5375	lt tan
△	760			3069	pink
◇	761			3068	lt pink
✕	762			8510	vy lt grey
•	310				black French Knot

The design was stitched over an 11" x 12" piece of 8.5 mesh waste canvas on a light blue sweatshirt. Six strands of floss were used for Cross Stitch, 2 strands for Backstitch, and 4 strands for French Knots. A bow tied from ¹/₁₆" ribbon was tacked under bear's chin.

Design by Kathie Rueger.

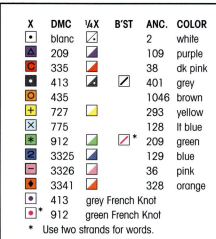

Our happy designs will turn tiny totes into fun gift bags in a snap. Fill them with colorful grass and bite-size candy for cute little favors or egg-hunt prizes!

X	DMC	¼X	B'ST	ANC.	COLOR
•	blanc			2	white
▲	209			109	purple
C	335			38	dk pink
◆	413		╱	401	grey
O	435			1046	brown
+	727			293	yellow
✕	775			128	lt blue
✱	912		╱ *	209	green
2	3325			129	blue
−	3326			36	pink
◆	3341			328	orange
•	413			grey French Knot	
• *	912			green French Knot	
*	Use two strands for words.				

Each design was stitched on an Ivory Lil' Tote (14 ct). Three strands of floss were used for Cross Stitch and 1 for Backstitch and French Knots, unless otherwise noted in color key.

Designs by Ann Townsend.

Easter fun is all lined up when you wear this "egg-cellent" shirt. For a playful touch, a holiday hare makes a surprise appearance amid the colorful eggs.

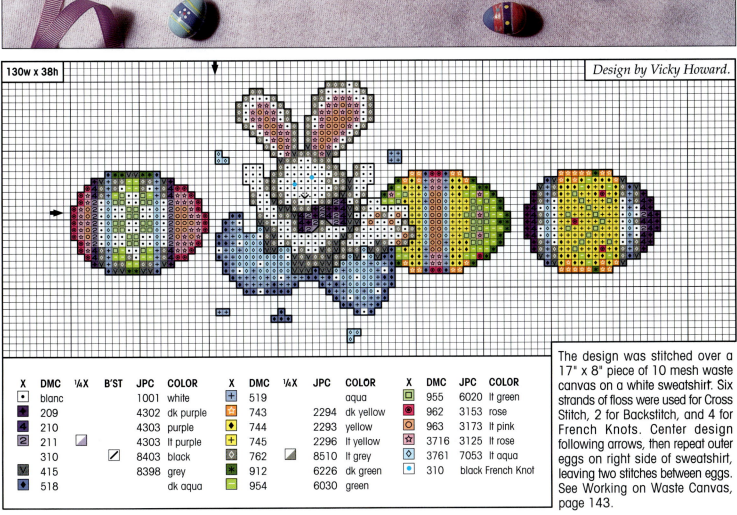

130w x 38h

Design by Vicky Howard.

X	DMC	1/4X	B'ST	JPC	COLOR
•	blanc			1001	white
◆	209			4302	dk purple
▲	210			4303	purple
2	211	◢		4303	lt purple
	310		◢	8403	black
∇	415				grey
◆	518			8398	dk aqua

X	DMC	1/4X	JPC	COLOR
+	519			aqua
☆	743		2294	dk yellow
◆	744		2293	yellow
+	745		2296	lt yellow
◇	762	◢	8510	lt grey
✳	912		6226	dk green
▣	954		6030	green

X	DMC	JPC	COLOR
▢	955	6020	lt green
◉	962	3153	rose
○	963	3173	lt pink
★	3716	3125	lt rose
◇	3761	7053	lt aqua
•	310		black French Knot

The design was stitched over a 17" x 8" piece of 10 mesh waste canvas on a white sweatshirt. Six strands of floss were used for Cross Stitch, 2 for Backstitch, and 4 for French Knots. Center design following arrows, then repeat outer eggs on right side of sweatshirt, leaving two stitches between eggs. See Working on Waste Canvas, page 143.

Easter is a time to celebrate new beginnings — spring flowers are blooming, green leaves and grass are sprouting, and lots of newborn animals are arriving. To honor the little ones in your life, stitch some of these winsome motifs on accessories for baby.

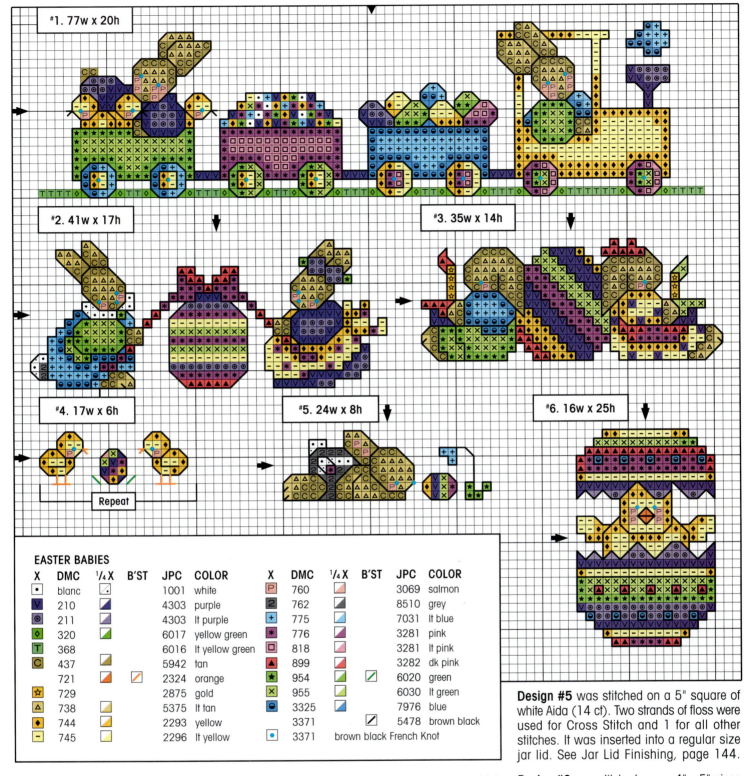

EASTER BABIES

X	DMC	1/4 X	B'ST	JPC	COLOR	X	DMC	1/4 X	B'ST	JPC	COLOR
•	blanc			1001	white	P	760			3069	salmon
V	210			4303	purple	2	762			8510	grey
◉	211			4303	lt purple	+	775			7031	lt blue
◇	320			6017	yellow green	*	776			3281	pink
T	368			6016	lt yellow green	□	818			3281	lt pink
C	437			5942	tan	▲	899			3282	dk pink
	721			2324	orange	★	954			6020	green
☆	729			2875	gold	×	955			6030	lt green
△	738			5375	lt tan	◉	3325			7976	blue
◆	744			2293	yellow		3371			5478	brown black
−	745			2296	lt yellow	•	3371				brown black French Knot

(**Note:** For waste canvas projects, see Working on Waste Canvas, page 143.)

Design #1 was stitched on the Aida (14 ct) insert of a white baby bib. Two strands of floss were used for Cross Stitch and 1 for all other stitches.

Design #2 was stitched on a white Aida (14 ct) baby bib. Two strands of floss were used for Cross Stitch and 1 for all other stitches. Tie a 10" length of 1/8"w ribbon into a bow; trim ends. Attach bow to bib.

Design #3 was stitched over a 5" x 4" piece of 14 mesh waste canvas on a pink baby T-shirt. Three strands of floss were used for Cross Stitch and 1 for all other stitches.

Design #4 was stitched three times over an 8" x 3" piece of 10 mesh waste canvas on a blue baby T-shirt. Four strands of floss were used for Cross Stitch, 2 for orange backstitch, and 1 for all other stitches.

Design #5 was stitched on a 5" square of white Aida (14 ct). Two strands of floss were used for Cross Stitch and 1 for all other stitches. It was inserted into a regular size jar lid. See Jar Lid Finishing, page 144.

Design #6 was stitched over a 4" x 5" piece of 14 mesh waste canvas on a yellow baby T-shirt. Three strands of floss were used for Cross Stitch and 1 for all other stitches.

Designs by Lorraine Birmingham.

Who says mugs are just for hot drinks? Stitched with one of our old-fashioned bunny designs and filled with candy, these mugs make cute Easter "baskets."

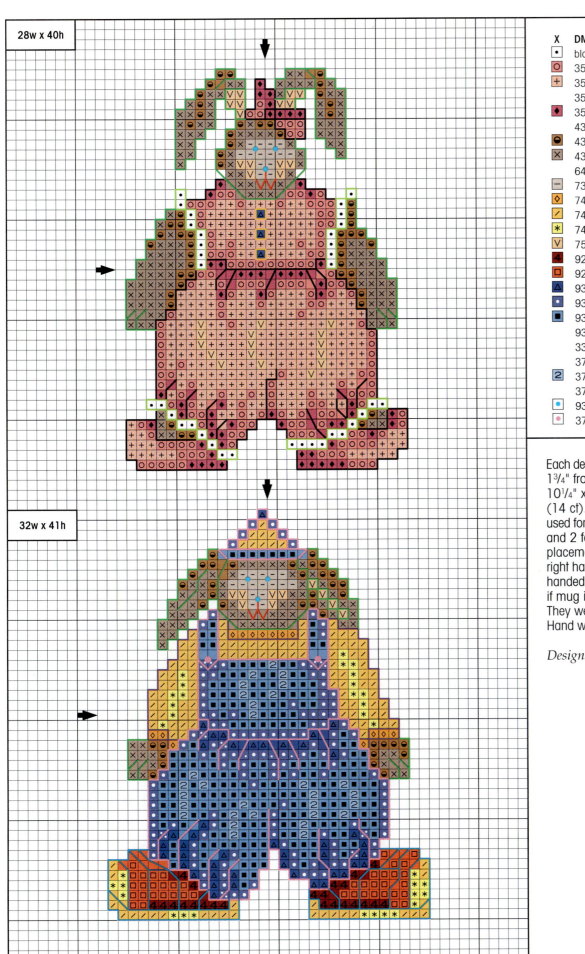

X	DMC	B'ST	JPC	COLOR
•	blanc		1001	white
○	352		3008	peach
+	353		3006	lt peach
	355	╱	2339	salmon
◆	356		2338	dk salmon
	434	╱	5000	brown
☺	436		5943	dk tan
✕	437		5942	tan
	640	╱	5393	beige
−	738		5375	lt tan
◇	744		2293	yellow
╱	745		2296	lt yellow
✳	746		2275	vy lt yellow
V	754		2331	vy lt peach
4	920		3337	rust
▢	921			lt rust
▲	930	╱	7052	dk blue
•	931		7051	blue
■	932		7050	lt blue
	938	╱	5477	dk brown
	3371	╱	5478	black brown
	3750	╱		vy dk blue
2	3752		7876	vy lt blue
	3790	╱		dk beige
●	938			dk brown French Knot
●	3750			vy dk blue French Knot

28w x 40h

32w x 41h

Each design was centered and stitched 1¾" from one short edge of a 10¼" x 3½" piece of Vinyl-Weave® (14 ct). Three strands of floss were used for Cross Stitch, 1 for Backstitch, and 2 for French Knots. For design placement, center mug design on right half of vinyl if mug is for a right-handed person or on left half of vinyl if mug is for a left-handed person. They were inserted in white mugs. Hand wash mugs to protect stitchery.

Designs by Sandy Gervais.

A wreath embellished with this whimsical design is a sweet way to greet your holiday guests. Encouraging company to "hop on in," the frolicsome bunnies set the tone for a lighthearted celebration.

HOP ON IN (112w x 93h)

X	DMC	¼X	B'ST	ANC	COLOR	X	DMC	¼X	ANC	COLOR
•	blanc			2	white	◆	801		359	dk brown
◇	ecru			387	ecru	●	930		1035	dk blue
◖	209			109	lavender	V	931		1034	blue
◉	223			895	lt mauve	×	932		1033	lt blue
▣	224			893	vy lt mauve	∗	993		186	aqua
	310		╱	403	black	–	3716		25	lt pink
	319		╱ *	218	green	★	3721		869	dk mauve
▲	436			1045	lt brown	▨	3722		1027	mauve
▨	738			361	tan	●	310			black French Knot
☆	739			387	lt tan					
⊙	743			302	lt yellow			* Use long, loose stitches.			

The design was stitched on a 16" x 15" piece of Light Blue Aida (14 ct). Three strands of floss were used for Cross Stitch and 1 for Backstitch and French Knots. It was inserted in a purchased frame (8" x 10" opening) and attached to a grapevine wreath. For wreath, spray paint wreath white. Glue Easter grass to inside of wreath to make a nest. Glue plastic eggs inside nest. Add curling ribbon and a wire-edged ribbon bow as desired. Glue framed stitched piece to wreath.

Design by Kathy Rueger.
Needlework adaptation by Christine Street and Jane Chandler.

PATRiOTiC DAYS

Colorful parades, lavish picnics, and spectacular displays of fireworks on July 4th and other patriotic days are grand American traditions! This star-spangled collection will inspire you to join in the festivities to honor those who have served our country. You'll find spirited T-shirts, along with a host of all-American accents for your home — all saluting the good old U.S.A.

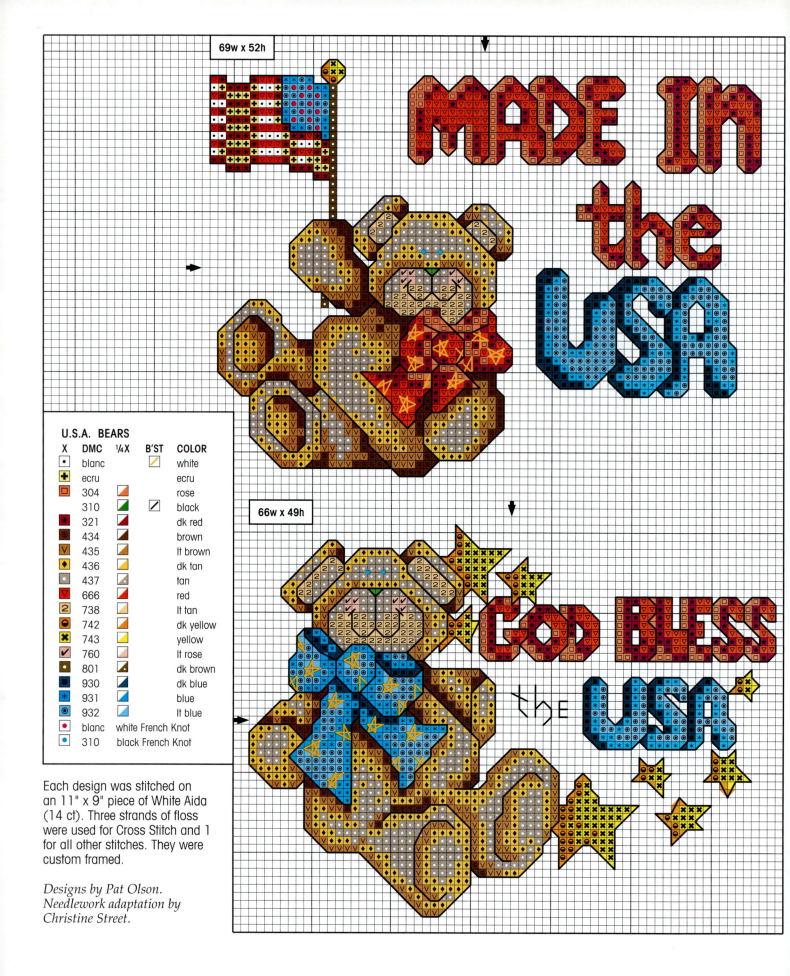

69w x 52h

66w x 49h

U.S.A. BEARS

X	DMC	¼X	B'ST	COLOR
•	blanc		/	white
+	ecru			ecru
▣	304			rose
	310		/	black
★	321			dk red
✛	434			brown
V	435			lt brown
◆	436			dk tan
▢	437			tan
▽	666			red
2	738			lt tan
⊙	742			dk yellow
✖	743			yellow
✔	760			lt rose
◉	801			dk brown
■	930			dk blue
✳	931			blue
◉	932			lt blue
●	blanc			white French Knot
•	310			black French Knot

Each design was stitched on an 11" x 9" piece of White Aida (14 ct). Three strands of floss were used for Cross Stitch and 1 for all other stitches. They were custom framed.

Designs by Pat Olson. Needlework adaptation by Christine Street.

This banner-waving bunch brightens a fingertip towel for the patriotic days of summer.

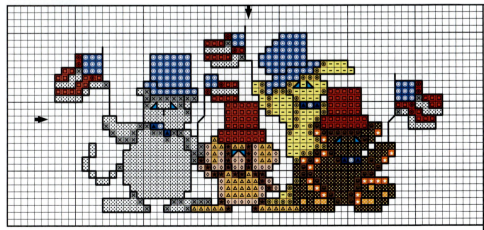

FLAG-WAVING FRIENDS (57w x 27h)					
X	DMC	¼X	¾X	B'ST	ANC.	COLOR
	blanc				2	white
	310				403	black
	321				9046	red
	433				358	dk brown
	434				310	brown
	435				1046	lt brown
	437				362	dk tan
	666				46	lt red
	738				361	tan
	739				387	lt tan
	762				234	grey
	796				133	dk blue
	797				132	blue
	3022				393	dk taupe
	3023					taupe
	3024				397	lt taupe

The design was stitched on the 14 ct insert of a white fingertip towel. Three strands of floss were used for Cross Stitch and 1 for Backstitch.

Design by Karen Wood.

The familiar words of our nation's Pledge of Allegiance bear witness to the story of how America was established on religious freedom. This handsome cross stitch design is a salute to our founding fathers.

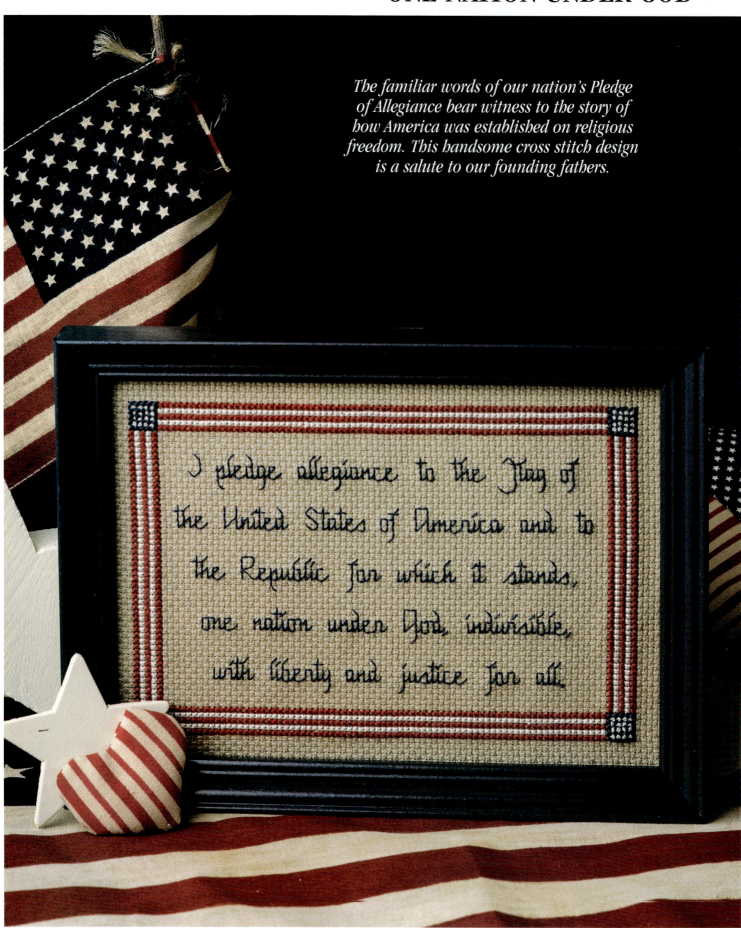

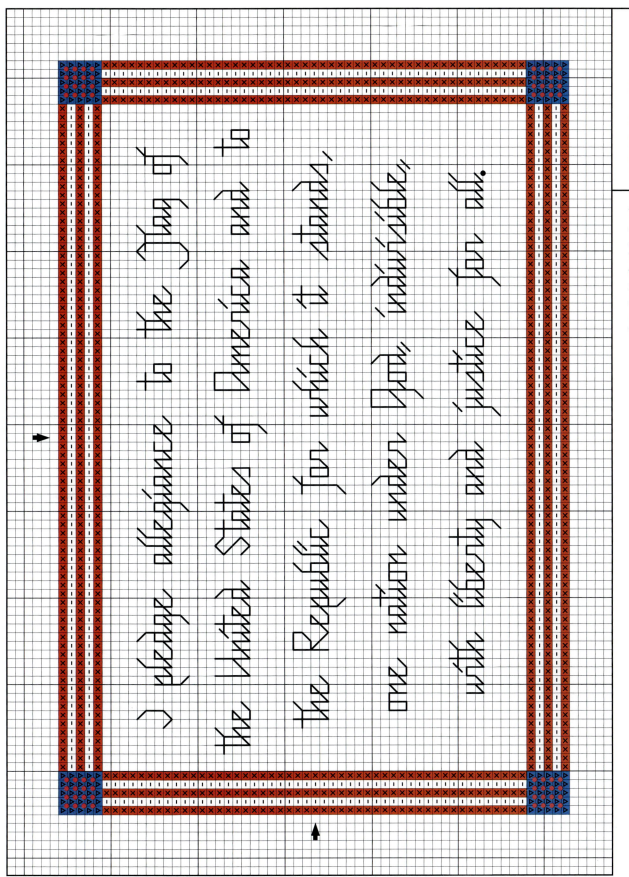

The design was stitched on an 11" x 9" piece of Dirty Aida (14 ct). Two strands of floss were used for Cross Stitch and 1 for all other stitches. It was inserted in a dark blue frame (5" x 7" opening).

49

Parade around in this crowd-pleasing shirt on the Fourth of July and you'll get three cheers for good taste!

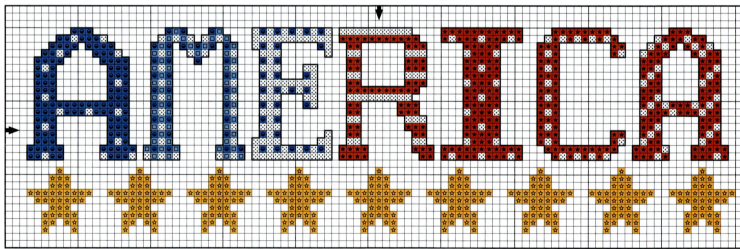

The design was stitched over a 16" x 8" piece of 8.5 mesh waste canvas on a white sweatshirt. Six strands of floss were used for Cross Stitch and 2 strands for Backstitch. See Working on Waste Canvas, page 143.

Design by Polly Carbonari.

AMERICA (97w x 28h)				
X	DMC	B'ST	ANC.	COLOR
⊠	blanc		2	white
	310	╱	403	black
★	321		9046	red
☆	783		307	gold
■	824		164	blue
▣	826		161	lt blue

This bread cloth is a reminder that our American heritage is just one of the many blessings God has bestowed on us.

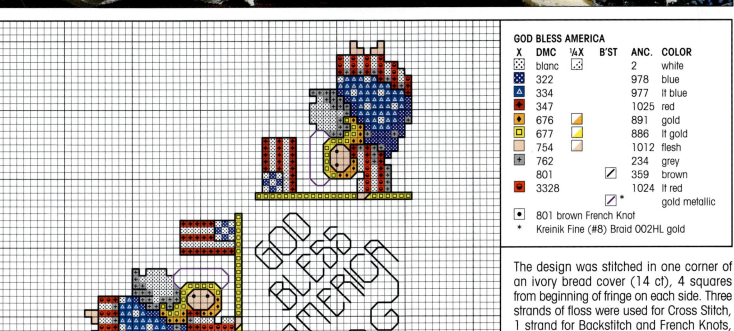

GOD BLESS AMERICA

X	DMC	¼X	B'ST	ANC.	COLOR
⊡	blanc	⊡		2	white
◼	322			978	blue
△	334			977	lt blue
◆	347			1025	red
◆	676	◢		891	gold
▢	677	◢		886	lt gold
▨	754	◢		1012	flesh
+	762			234	grey
	801		╱	359	brown
◉	3328			1024	lt red
			╱ *		gold metallic
◉	801 brown French Knot				
*	Kreinik Fine (#8) Braid 002HL gold				

The design was stitched in one corner of an ivory bread cover (14 ct), 4 squares from beginning of fringe on each side. Three strands of floss were used for Cross Stitch, 1 strand for Backstitch and French Knots, and 1 strand for gold metallic Backstitch.

Design by Deborah Lambein.

These insulated beverage holders are too cool! Not only do they keep your drinks cold when summer heats up, but they display our national colors and symbols, too.

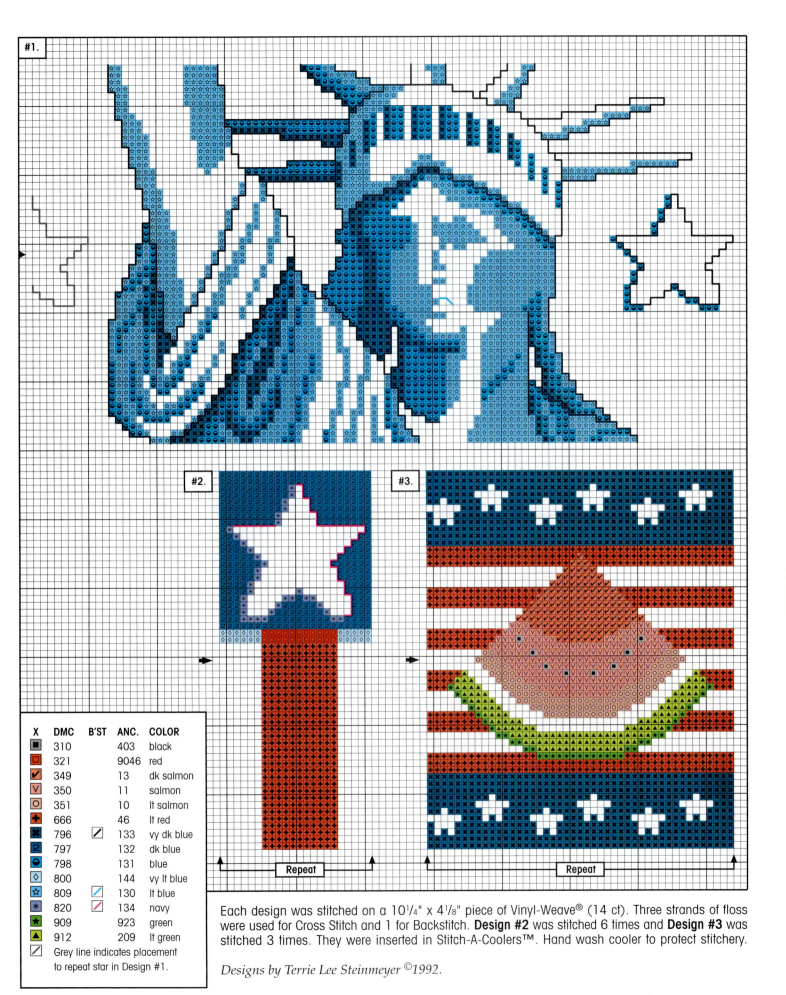

X	DMC	B'ST	ANC.	COLOR
■	310		403	black
□	321		9046	red
✔	349		13	dk salmon
▽	350		11	salmon
○	351		10	lt salmon
✚	666		46	lt red
✖	796	╱	133	vy dk blue
2	797		132	dk blue
◐	798		131	blue
◇	800		144	vy lt blue
☆	809	╱	130	lt blue
✳	820	╱	134	navy
★	909		923	green
▲	912		209	lt green
╱	Grey line indicates placement to repeat star in Design #1.			

Each design was stitched on a 10¼" x 4⅛" piece of Vinyl-Weave® (14 ct). Three strands of floss were used for Cross Stitch and 1 for Backstitch. **Design #2** was stitched 6 times and **Design #3** was stitched 3 times. They were inserted in Stitch-A-Coolers™. Hand wash cooler to protect stitchery.

Designs by Terrie Lee Steinmeyer ©1992.

Our country was settled by pioneers such as John Chapman, more commonly known as Johnny Appleseed. This folksy pillow pays tribute to the man who devoted his life to planting apple trees along the frontier.

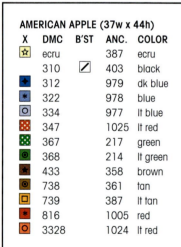

X	DMC	B'ST	ANC.	COLOR
☆	ecru		387	ecru
	310	╱	403	black
	312		979	dk blue
	322		978	blue
	334		977	lt blue
	347		1025	lt red
	367		217	green
	368		214	lt green
	433		358	brown
	738		361	tan
	739		387	lt tan
	816		1005	red
	3328		1024	lt red

AMERICAN APPLE (37w x 44h)

The design was stitched on an 8" square of Ivory Aida (14 ct). Three strands of floss were used for Cross Stitch and 1 strand for Backstitch. It was made into a pillow. See Apple Pillow Finishing, page 144.

Design by Ursula Wollenberg.

With our stars and stripes alphabet, you can create a closetful of flag-waving gear. "Made in America" is a darling phrase for a little one's tee.

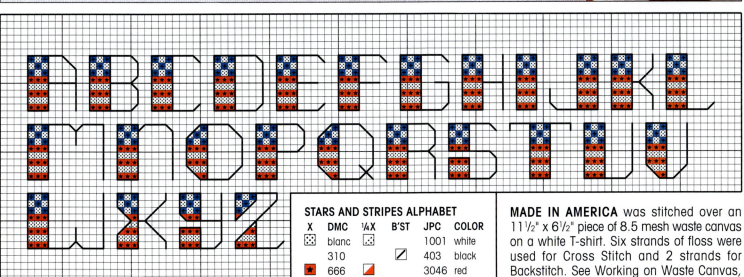

STARS AND STRIPES ALPHABET				
X	DMC	1/4X	B'ST	JPC	COLOR
⊠	blanc	⋅		1001	white
	310		╱	403	black
★	666		╱	3046	red
✛	824		◹	7182	blue

MADE IN AMERICA was stitched over an 11½" x 6½" piece of 8.5 mesh waste canvas on a white T-shirt. Six strands of floss were used for Cross Stitch and 2 strands for Backstitch. See Working on Waste Canvas, page 143.

Holding a lighted sparkler and an American flag, these star-spangled angels are the image of loyal patriots. We fashioned the pair into pillows.

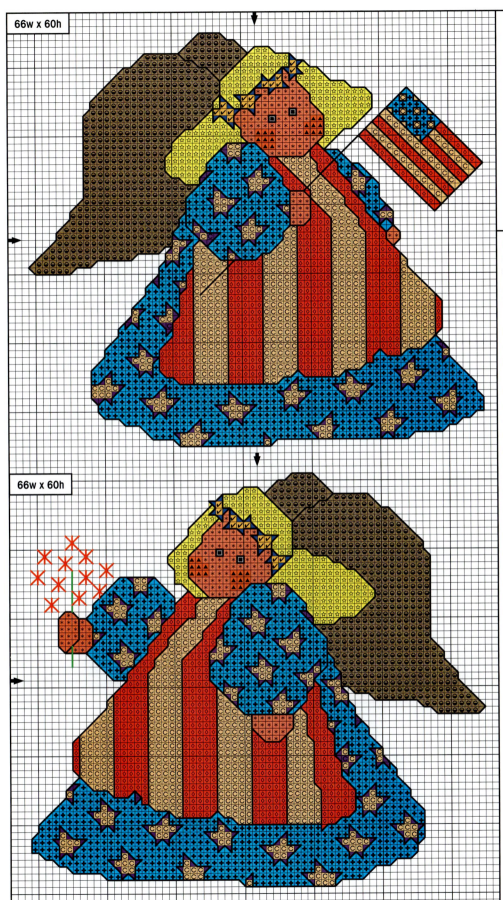

66w x 60h

66w x 60h

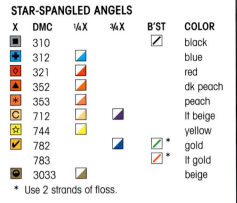

STAR-SPANGLED ANGELS

X	DMC	1/4X	3/4X	B'ST	COLOR
■	310			∕	black
✚	312	◣			blue
◆	321	◣			red
▲	352	◣			dk peach
✱	353	◣			peach
C	712	◣	◣		lt beige
★	744	◣			yellow
✔	782		◣	∕ *	gold
	783			∕ *	lt gold
◕	3033	◣			beige

* Use 2 strands of floss.

Each design was stitched on a 9" square of Smoke Aida (14 ct). Three strands of floss were used for Cross Stitch and 1 for Backstitch (unless otherwise indicated in the color key). They were made into pillows.

For each pillow, trim stitched piece 1¼" larger than the design on all sides. Cut a piece of fabric the same size as the stitched piece for backing.

For cording, cut one 2" x 27" bias strip of fabric and one 27" length of ¼" dia. purchased cord. Center cord on wrong side of bias strip; matching long edges, fold strip over cord. Using zipper foot, baste along length of strip close to cord; trim seam allowance to ½". Matching raw edges and beginning at bottom edge, pin cording to right side of stitched piece, making a ³⁄₈" clip in seam allowance of cording at each corner. Ends of cording should overlap approximately 2"; pin overlapping end out of the way. Starting 2" from beginning end of cording and ending 4" from overlapping end, sew cording to stitched piece. On overlapping end of cording, remove 2½" of basting; fold end of fabric back and trim cord so it meets beginning end of cord. Fold end of fabric under ½"; wrap fabric over beginning end of cording. Finish sewing cording to stitched piece.

For ruffle, press short ends of a 4½" x 51" strip of fabric ½" to wrong side. Matching wrong sides and long edges, fold strip in half; press. Gather fabric strip to fit stitched piece. Matching raw edges and beginning at bottom edge, pin ruffle to right side of stitched piece, overlapping short ends ¼". Using a ½" seam allowance, sew ruffle to stitched piece. Matching right sides and leaving an opening for turning, use a ½" seam allowance to sew stitched piece and backing fabric together. Trim corners diagonally. Turn pillow right side out, carefully pushing corners outward. Stuff pillow with polyester fiberfill and whipstitch opening closed.

Designs by Sharon Barrett.

57

This quick-and-easy bread cloth will add a bit of red, white, and blue spirit to all your summer celebrations.

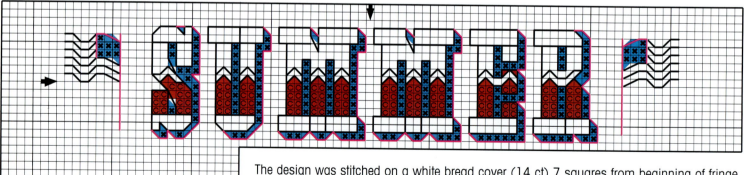

SUMMER (77w x 14h)					
X	DMC	¼X	B'ST	ANC.	COLOR
C	347			1025	red
X	796			133	blue

The design was stitched on a white bread cover (14 ct) 7 squares from beginning of fringe. Two strands of floss were used for Cross Stitch and 1 for Backstitch.

To finish corners of bread cover, cut a 3" square out of each corner. Machine stitch ½" from raw edges; clip inner corners diagonally to machine-stitched lines. Fringe fabric to machine-stitched lines.

Design by Nancy Spruance.

Show your pride in America with our spectacular mug. The bold cup commemorates a glorious day in our nation's history.

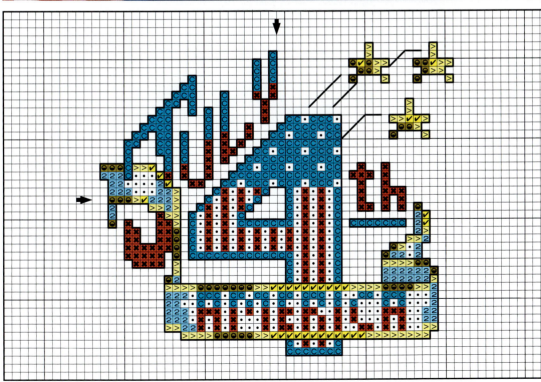

JULY 4TH (44w x 39h)

X	DMC	B'ST	ANC.	COLOR
•	blanc		2	white
	310	∕	403	black
✖	666		46	red
✔	725		305	yellow
>	726		295	lt yellow
⊖	783		307	dk yellow
C	797		132	blue
2	3753		1031	lt blue

The design was stitched on a 10½" x 3½" piece of Vinyl-Weave® (14 ct). Three strands of floss were used for Cross Stitch and 1 for Backstitch. Place design on vinyl 1½" from desired short edge and ³/₈" from the bottom edge. Place vinyl in mug with short edges aligned with handle. Hand wash mug to protect stitchery.

Design by Barbara Baatz, Kooler Design Studio.

Make your guests feel welcome with this heartwarming pillow. The flag-inspired motif can also be used to create lots of decorative accents, such as our homespun heartstring of mini pillows.

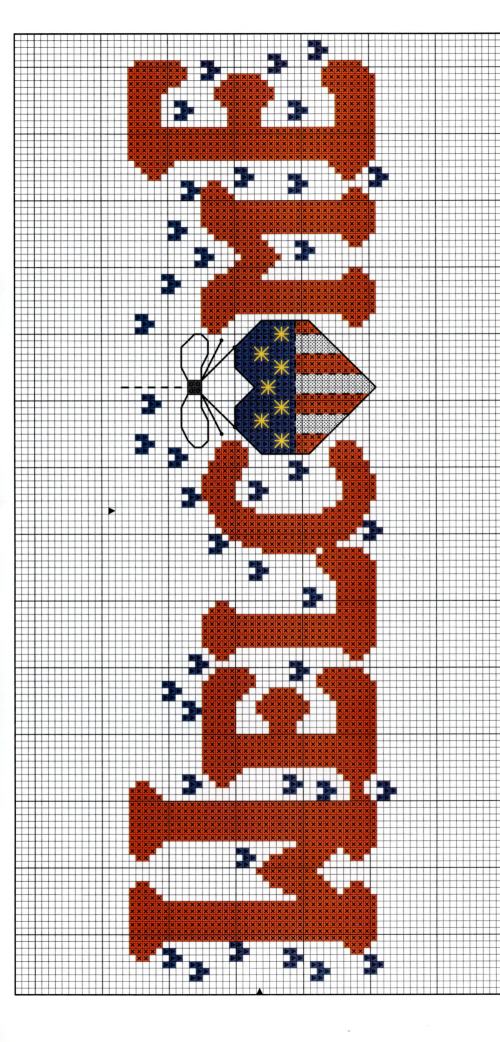

The design was stitched on a 12⅛" x 4⅛" piece of Dirty Aida (14 ct). Three strands of floss were used for Cross Stitch and 1 for all other stitches. It was made into a pillow.

For pillow, cut backing fabric (same fabric as stitched piece) same size as the stitched piece. Matching wrong sides, use desired floss color to work running stitch (over and under 2 fabric threads) ½" from top and bottom edges and one side edge. Stuff pillow with polyester fiberfill. Continue working running stitches across remaining side of pillow ½" from edge. Fringe fabric to one square from running stitches.

The **heart** only was stitched on a 2½" square of Dirty Aida (14 ct). Three strands of floss were used for Cross Stitch and 1 for Backstitch. The design was stitched twice and made into mini pillows.

For each mini pillow, cut backing fabric (same fabric as stitched piece) same size as the stitched piece. Matching wrong sides, use desired floss color to work running stitch (over and under 2 fabric threads) ½" from bottom and side edges. Stuff pillow with polyester fiberfill.

To hang pillows together, place one end of a 7" length of jute between fabric pieces at center top edge of each pillow. Catching ends of jute in stitching, continue working running stitches across top of pillow ½" from edge. Fringe fabric to one square from running stitches.

Design by Kathie Rueger.

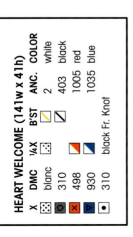

HEART WELCOME (141w x 41h)

X	DMC	ANC.	COLOR	¼X	B'ST
	blanc	2	white		
	310	403	black		
	498	1005	red		
	930	1035	blue		
	310		black Fr. Knot		

HALLOWEEN

*F*rom ghoulies and ghosties, long-leggity beasties, and things that go bump in the night, Good Lord deliver us! This haunting Halloween collection of "spook-tacular" designs includes everything you need to make the night unforgettable. You'll find lots of hair-raising designs such as the ones shown here, plus spooky socks and sweatshirts, trick-or-treat mugs and totes, and some "boo-tiful" accents for your home. Making mischief has never been easier — or more fun!

X	DMC	¼X	B'ST	ANC.
•	blanc			2
◼	310			403
◉	414			235
★	437			362
◒	704			256
◈	725			305
◼	776			24
✕	947			330
−	970			316
•	310	black French Knot		

Designs by Carol Boswell.

The **Boo** design was stitched on the 14 ct insert of a black fingertip towel. Four strands of floss were used for Cross Stitch, 2 for 704 and 414 Backstitch, and 1 for all other stitches.

The **Cat** design was stitched on a 10½" x 3½" piece of Vinyl-Weave® (14 ct). Borders were extended to the edges of vinyl. Three strands of floss were used for Cross Stitch, 2 for blanc Backstitch, and 1 for 310 Backstitch. It was inserted in a mug. Hand wash mug to protect stitchery.

The **Ghosts** design was stitched on a black bread cover (14 ct), four squares from beginning of fringe. Four strands of floss were used for Cross Stitch, 2 for 947 Backstitch, and 1 for all other stitches.

The **Witch** design was stitched on a 7" square of White Aida (16 ct). Two strands of floss were used for Cross Stitch and 1 for Backstitch. It was inserted in a wide-mouth jar lid. See Jar Lid Finishing, page 144.

The **Yo!** design was stitched over a 10" square of 8.5 waste canvas on a black sweatshirt. Seven strands of floss were used for Cross Stitch and 2 for Backstitch. See Working on Waste Canvas, page 143.

It's no trick — these totes are a real treat! Stitched on a large tote, this whimsical design dresses up a trick-or-treat bag for a youngster. To delight a friend, tuck a treat inside a mini tote adorned with one of these pumpkin pals. Either way, Halloween merry-making is in the bag!

TRICK OR TREAT (76w x 42h)

X	DMC	¼X	¾X	B'ST	COLOR
	blanc			╱	white
■	310			╱	black
◆	347		◢	╱	red
▽	435		◢		lt brown
★	720				dk orange
=	740	◰			vy lt orange
⊠	791		◣		blue
◨	801				brown
◉	947				orange
✳	971	◰			lt orange
▲	3345			╱	green

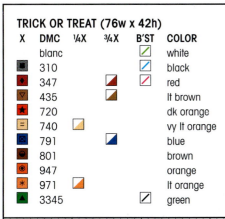

The design was stitched on the 6 ct insert of a tote bag. Nine strands of floss were used for Cross Stitch and 6 for Backstitch.

Each pumpkin design was stitched on an Ivory Lil' Tote (14 ct) over two fabric threads. Six strands of floss were used for Cross Stitch and 2 for Backstitch.

Design by Anne Elmore.

Perched on the moon, a playful witch embellishes this cozy sweatshirt. It's perfect to wear when you're escorting young trick-or-treaters or attending an All Hallows' Eve bash!

79w x 80h

X	DMC	B'ST	ANC.	COLOR	X	DMC	B'ST	ANC.	COLOR
★	208		110	dk lavender	>	741		304	dk yellow
□	209		109	lavender	✖	742		303	yellow
✚	210		108	lt lavender	⊠	743	/	302	lt yellow
✦	211		342	vy lt lavender	4	754		1012	peach
	310	/	403	black	∏	900		333	rust
✳	353		6	dk peach	2	946		332	dk orange
▲	434		310	brown	♥	947		330	orange
◉	435		1046	lt brown	T	948		1011	lt peach
✫	550		102	dk purple	✜	970		316	lt orange
◤	552		99	purple	%	3825			vy lt orange
⊟	553		98	lt purple	○	947			orange French Knot
•	554		96	vy lt purple					

The design was stitched over a 14" square of 8.5 mesh waste canvas on a black sweatshirt. Six strands of floss were used for Cross Stitch and 2 for Backstitch and French Knots. The design was centered horizontally 1½" from the bottom of the neckband. See Working on Waste Canvas, page 143.

Design by Pat Olson.
Needlework adaptation by Jane Chandler.

"BEARY" FUN TOTES

Our cute mini totes are the ideal way to treat your favorite tricksters to a batch of devilishly delicious snack mix. Even when the munchies are gone, the bags will still bring squeals of delight!

Each design was stitched on an Ivory Lil' Tote (14 ct). Three strands of floss were used for Cross Stitch and 1 for Backstitch and French Knots.

Designs by Lorraine Birmingham.

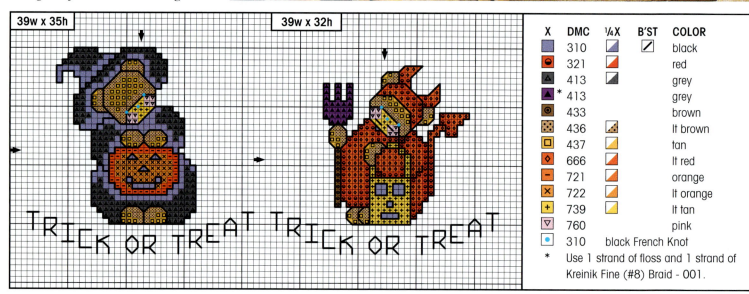

X	DMC	¼X	B'ST	COLOR
■	310	◪	╱	black
⊙	321	◪		red
▲	413	◪	◪	grey
▲*	413			grey
◉	433			brown
⬚	436	◪		lt brown
□	437	◪		tan
◇	666	◪		lt red
−	721	◪		orange
✕	722	◪		lt orange
+	739	◪		lt tan
▽	760			pink
•	310			black French Knot
*				Use 1 strand of floss and 1 strand of Kreinik Fine (#8) Braid - 001.

39w x 35h

39w x 32h

Perfect for serving up a cup of savory Halloween brew, this cute mug depicts a little girl dressed up like a pumpkin.

PUMPKIN GIRL (30w x 40h)

X	DMC	B'ST	ANC.	COLOR		X	DMC	B'ST	ANC.	COLOR
●	310	⟋	403	black		✳	840		379	lt brown
△	436		1045	tan		✦	844		1041	grey
⊙	720		326	dk orange		✛	948		1011	peach
✕	721		324	orange		◉	3346		267	green
−	722		323	lt orange		▽	3347		266	lt green
◇	761		1021	pink		●	310			black French Knot
★	839		360	brown						

The design was stitched on a 10½" x 3½" piece of Vinyl-Weave® (14 ct). Three strands of floss were used for Cross Stitch and 1 for Backstitch and French Knots. It was inserted in a black mug. Hand wash mug to protect stitchery.

Design by Sandy Gervais.
Needlework adaptation by Jane Chandler.

There'll be mischief afoot when you don these spooky socks. The ten designs are so bewitching, you'll be tempted to make all of them!

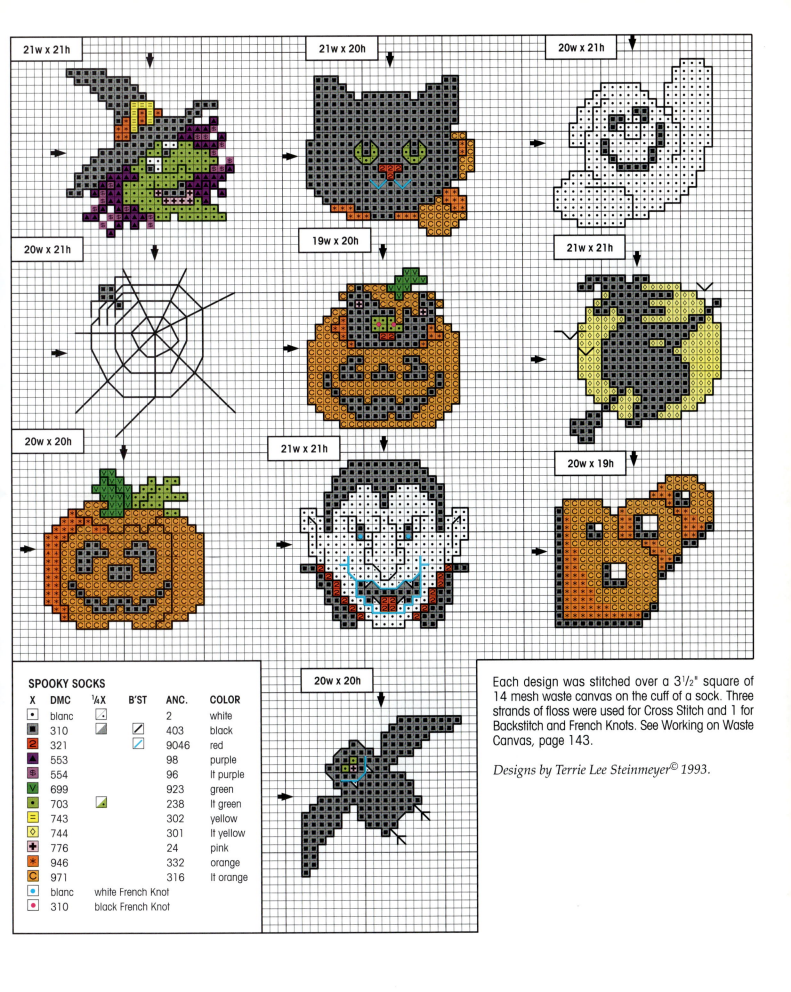

SPOOKY SOCKS

X	DMC	¼X	B'ST	ANC.	COLOR
·	blanc			2	white
■	310		/	403	black
2	321		/	9046	red
▲	553			98	purple
$	554			96	lt purple
V	699			923	green
•	703			238	lt green
=	743			302	yellow
◇	744			301	lt yellow
+	776			24	pink
*	946			332	orange
C	971			316	lt orange
•	blanc		white French Knot		
•	310		black French Knot		

Each design was stitched over a 3½" square of 14 mesh waste canvas on the cuff of a sock. Three strands of floss were used for Cross Stitch and 1 for Backstitch and French Knots. See Working on Waste Canvas, page 143.

Designs by Terrie Lee Steinmeyer© 1993.

71

With our wicked witch and her friends on hand, you're sure to brew up a batch of Halloween cheer! For a haunting good time, stitch these monstrous motifs on a sweatshirt, or use them to dress up a little bag of treats. The black cat is just right to top off a jar of goodies.

from ghoulies
and ghosties,
long-leggity beasties,
and things that go
bump in
the night,
Good Lord
deliver us.

85w x 117h

from ghostes
and ghosties,
long-leggity beasties,
and things that go
bump in
the night,
Good Lord
deliver us.

The **Witch and Friends** design was stitched on a 15" x 17" piece of White Aida (14 ct). Two strands of floss were used for Cross Stitch and 1 for Backstitch and French Knots. It was custom framed.

The **Witch, Crow, and Ghost** were stitched over a 10" x 9" piece of 12 mesh waste canvas on a white sweatshirt. Three strands of floss were used for Cross Stitch and 1 for Backstitch and French Knots. See Working on Waste Canvas, page 143.

The **Witch and Crow** were stitched on an 8" x 11½" piece of White Aida (14 ct). The design was centered and stitched with the bottom of design 2¼" from one short edge of fabric. Two strands of floss were used for Cross Stitch and 1 for Backstitch and French Knots. It was made into a treat bag.

For bag, cut a second piece of Aida same size as stitched piece for backing. Fold a 36" length of ³⁄₈"w ribbon in half. On right side of stitched piece, 2½" from top, pin folded edge of ribbon even with left raw edge. Place right sides of fabrics together. Beginning and ending seam ½" from top edge, sew fabric together along sides and bottom edge using a ½" seam allowance. Turn bag right side out and fringe top edge ½".

The **Cat** was stitched on an 8" x 7" piece of White Aida (18 ct). Two strands of floss were used for Cross Stitch and 1 for Backstitch and French Knots. It was inserted in a wide-mouth jar lid. See Jar Lid Finishing, page 144.

Design by Kathie Rueger.

X	DMC	¼X	B'ST	ANC	COLOR	X	DMC	¼X	ANC	COLOR	X	DMC	¼X	B'ST	ANC	COLOR
•	blanc			2	white	✖	605		50	pink	=	726			295	lt yellow
✚	310			403	black	▲	666		46	red	◖	762			234	vy lt grey
2	317			400	dk grey	★	702		226	dk green	◉	947			330	orange
◆	413			401	vy dk grey	◇	703		238	green	•	310				black French Knot
▽	414			235	grey	$	704		256	lt green	•	762				vy lt grey French Knot
4	415			398	lt grey	∨	725		305	yellow						

73

Here's a sampling of motifs that's sure to get you in the spirit. Featuring candy corn, a ghost, and some pumpkin-patch pals, the designs offer a creepy collection of characters to cover you from head to toe!

48w x 17h

56w x 14h

28w x 28h

20w x 31h

HALLOWEEN WEAR

X	DMC	¼X	B'ST	ANC.	COLOR
•	blanc			2	white
■	310	◩	◩ *	403	black
◆	320	◩		215	green
★	367	◩		217	dk green
✳	644	◩		830	dk beige
•	676	◩		891	lt gold
✳	680			901	dk gold
+	729	◩		890	gold
▽	822	◩		390	beige
◣	839	◩		360	brown
◕	919			340	dk orange
✕	921	◩		1003	orange
◦	922	◩		1003	lt orange
●	310				black French Knot

* Use 2 strands of floss for letters.

Note: For waste canvas projects, see Working on Waste Canvas, page 143. For stiffened projects, see Stiffened Item Finishing, page 144. Refer to the photo for placement of the designs on projects.

The **Candy Corn** and **Words and Star** designs were stitched over 11 mesh waste canvas on a purchased chambray shirt. Four strands of floss were used for Cross Stitch and 1 for Backstitch.

The **Pumpkins** were stitched over a 10" x 6" piece of 8.5 mesh waste canvas on a black sweatshirt. Six strands of floss were used for Cross Stitch and 2 for Backstitch.

One **Pumpkin** was stitched on a 4" square of Ivory Aida (11 ct). Four strands of floss were used for Cross Stitch and 1 for Backstitch. It was stiffened and glued to the center of a purchased hairbow.

One **Pumpkin** was stitched twice on a 7" x 5" piece of Ivory Aida (11 ct) with 1" between designs. Four strands of floss were used for Cross Stitch and 1 for Backstitch. They were stiffened and a clip-on earring back was glued to the back of each stitched piece.

The **Ghost** was stitched on a 6" square of Ivory Aida (14 ct). Three strands of floss were used for Cross Stitch and 1 for Backstitch and French Knots. It was stiffened and a pin back was glued to the center back of the stitched piece.

Original artwork by Susan Fouts.
Needlework adaptation by Mike Vickery.

Your Halloween guests won't have to guess "witch" towel to use — these wacky witches and their black cats will attract them with their magical charms!

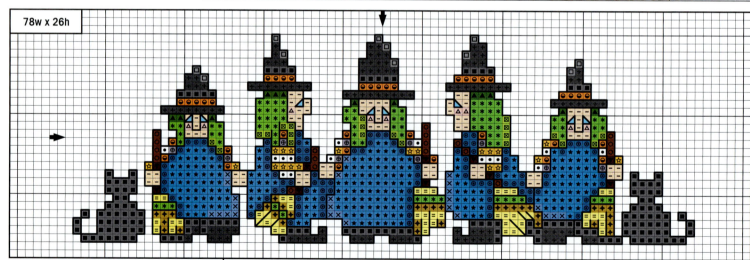

78w x 26h

The design was stitched on the 14 ct insert of a white fingertip towel. Three strands of floss were used for Cross Stitch and 1 for Backstitch.

Design by Karen Wood.

X	DMC	¾X	B'ST	ANC.	COLOR	X	DMC	¼X	ANC.	COLOR	X	DMC	ANC.	COLOR
•	blanc			2	white	*	702		226	green	★	798	131	blue
△	224			893	pink	⊠	703		238	lt green	✕	799	136	lt blue
■	310	◪	╱	403	black	⊟	725		305	yellow	⊙	947	330	orange
▢	413			401	grey	−	754	◱	1012	flesh	☆	971	316	lt orange
■	434			310	brown	⊕	762		234	lt grey	✦	3799	236	dk grey
■	435			1046	lt brown	✦	783		307	gold				
▲	701			227	dk green	⊙	797		132	dk blue				

You don't have to be a college student to enjoy this spooky sweatshirt! Frightfully fun to wear, the collegiate-style design has universal appeal. The bold colors and lettering make the quick-to-stitch shirt a real eye-catcher.

BOO U (50w x 55h)

X	DMC	¼X	B'ST	ANC	COLOR
	310		✓	403	black
+	318	◩		399	grey
★	413	◩		401	dk grey
✕	608	◪		332	orange
▲	762	◩		234	lt grey
O	973	◪		297	yellow

The design was stitched over a 10" x 11" piece of 8.5 mesh waste canvas on a white sweatshirt. Six strands of floss were used for Cross Stitch and 2 for Backstitch. See Working on Waste Canvas, page 143.

Design by Vicky Howard.

This haunting display features all our favorite Halloween symbols. The motifs are simply stitched and then finished with needlework stiffener to create enchanting ornaments.

ORNAMENTS

X	DMC	¼X	B'ST	ANC.	COLOR	X	DMC	¼X	ANC.	COLOR
•	blanc	◢		2	white	★	761		1021	pink
■	310		◢	403	black	◆	822	◢	390	ecru
	319		◢	218	dk green	✦	839	◢	360	brown
◆	356			5975	dk flesh	+	840	◢	379	taupe
⊖	367	◢		217	green	●	844	◢	1041	dk grey
×	415		◢	398	lt grey	●	920	◢	1004	dk rust
⊙	644		◢	830	beige	▼	921	◢	1003	rust
∨	645	◢		273	grey	◇	922	◢	1003	lt rust
▽	676	◢	◢	891	lt gold	2	948		1011	lt flesh
✱	729	◢		890	gold	•	310			black French Knot
4	754	◢		1012	flesh	•	761			pink French Knot

Each design was stitched on a 10" square of Ivory Aida (14 ct). Three strands of floss were used for Cross Stitch and 1 for Backstitch and French Knots. They were stiffened and made into ornaments.

For each ornament, cut a piece of muslin the same size as stitched piece for backing. Apply needlework stiffener to the back of stitched piece. Matching wrong sides, place stitched piece on backing fabric; allow to dry. Apply stiffener to muslin; allow to dry. Trim to within ½ square around edges of design. To prevent fraying, apply a small amount of stiffener to edges of design. For hanger, glue jute to back of the design as desired.

Designs by Susan Fouts.

Grinning jack-o'-lanterns, black cats, and ghosts unite to create this "spook-tacular" party set. The quick-to-stitch projects guarantee a ghoulishly good gathering!

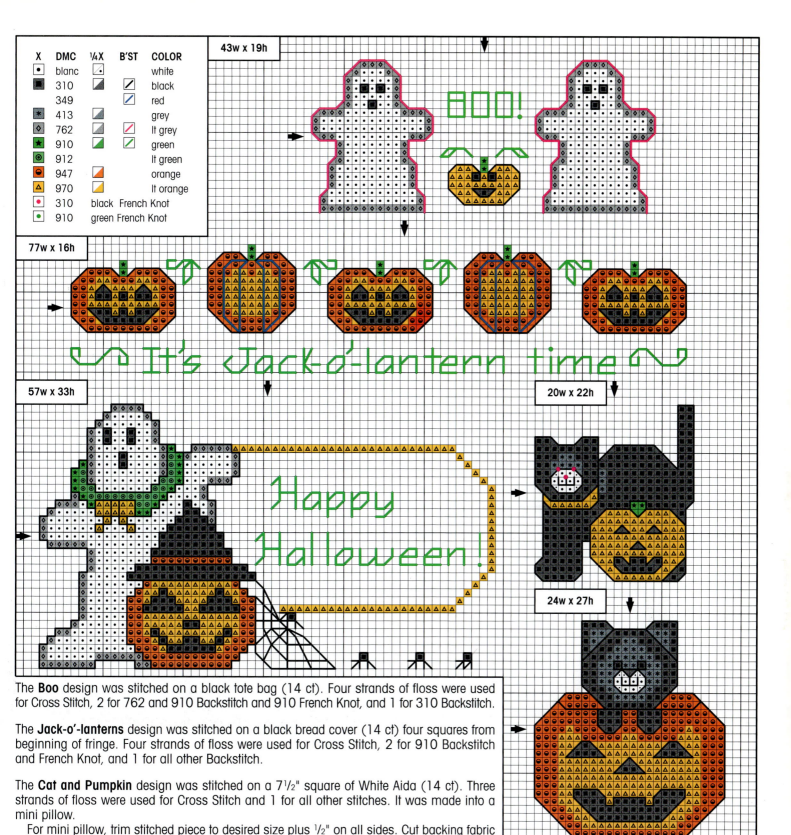

X	DMC	1/4X	B'ST	COLOR
•	blanc			white
■	310		/	black
	349		/	red
✱	413			grey
◆	762			lt grey
★	910		/	green
◉	912			lt green
■	947			orange
▲	970			lt orange
•	310			black French Knot
•	910			green French Knot

43w x 19h

BOO!

77w x 16h

It's Jack-o'-lantern time

57w x 33h

Happy Halloween!

20w x 22h

24w x 27h

The **Boo** design was stitched on a black tote bag (14 ct). Four strands of floss were used for Cross Stitch, 2 for 762 and 910 Backstitch and 910 French Knot, and 1 for 310 Backstitch.

The **Jack-o'-lanterns** design was stitched on a black bread cover (14 ct) four squares from beginning of fringe. Four strands of floss were used for Cross Stitch, 2 for 910 Backstitch and French Knot, and 1 for all other Backstitch.

The **Cat and Pumpkin** design was stitched on a 7 1/2" square of White Aida (14 ct). Three strands of floss were used for Cross Stitch and 1 for all other stitches. It was made into a mini pillow.

For mini pillow, trim stitched piece to desired size plus 1/2" on all sides. Cut backing fabric (same fabric as stitched piece) the same size as stitched piece. Matching wrong sides and raw edges, machine stitch fabric pieces together 1/2" from bottom and side edges. Stuff pillow with polyester fiberfill; machine stitch across top of pillow 1/2" from edge. Fringe fabric to within one square of machine-stitched lines.

The **Happy Halloween** design was stitched on a 10 1/2" x 3 1/2" piece of Vinyl-Weave® (14 ct). Three strands of floss were used for Cross Stitch, 2 for 910 Backstitch and French Knot, and 1 for 310 Backstitch. It was inserted in a black mug. Hand wash mug to protect stitchery.

The **Cat in Pumpkin** design was stitched on an 8" square of White Aida (14 ct). Three strands of floss were used for Cross Stitch and 1 for Backstitch. It was inserted in a small-mouth jar lid. See Jar Lid Finishing, page 144.

Designs by Ann Townsend.

Vintage postcards were the inspiration for this Halloween design. The coordinating accents were fashioned using motifs from the framed piece.

WITCH AND FRIENDS (77w x 71h)

X	DMC	¼X	½X	B'ST	ANC.	COLOR	X	DMC	¼X	ANC.	COLOR
■	310	◢		◿	403	black	✚	720	◸	326	dk orange
✳	347				1025	red	◢	721	◸	324	orange
$	413	◢			401	grey	✖	722		323	lt orange
▽	414	◢			235	lt grey	=	744	▢	301	yellow
★	420	◢			374	dk tan	%	754	◸	1012	lt peach
◉	422	◢			373	tan	◇	758		882	peach
▲	433				358	brown	⊠	761	◸	1021	pink
▼	434				310	lt brown	Ⅱ	935		861	dk green
	642		▣		392	grey brown	H	987		244	green
☆	676				891	gold	✳	989		242	lt green
⊙	677				886	lt gold	2	3328	◸	1024	lt red
✔	680				901	dk gold	•	310			black French Knot

The **Witch and Friends** design was stitched on a 9½" x 9" piece of Ivory Aida (14 ct). Three strands of floss were used for Cross Stitch, 1 for Half Cross Stitch and Backstitch, and 2 for French Knots. It was inserted in a purchased frame (7" square opening).

The **Pumpkins** on the left side of the design were each stitched over 2 fabric threads on a 5" square of Ivory Aida (14 ct). Six strands of floss were used for Cross stitch and 2 for Backstitch. Fill in area on right side of tall pumpkin as desired. They were stiffened and made into ornaments.

For each ornament, cut a piece of muslin the same size as stitched piece for backing. Apply needlework stiffener to the back of stitched piece. Matching wrong sides, place stitched piece on backing fabric; allow to dry. Apply stiffener to muslin; allow to dry. Trim to within ½ square around edges of design. To prevent fraying, apply a small amount of stiffener to edges of design.

The **Cat** and **Pumpkin** on the right side of the design were stitched over 2 fabric threads on an Ivory Lil' Tote (14 ct). Six strands of floss were used for Cross Stitch, 2 for Backstitch, and 4 for French Knots.

Design by Jacqueline Fox.

This friendly little ghost has brought along two pumpkin pals to help spell out his favorite Halloween greeting. Just right for holding a warm drink, the mug makes a spirited treat for a special friend.

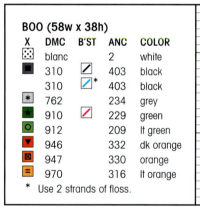

BOO (58w x 38h)

X	DMC	B'ST	ANC	COLOR
⊠	blanc		2	white
■	310	╱	403	black
	310	╱*	403	black
✳	762		234	grey
★	910	╱	229	green
○	912		209	lt green
▼	946		332	dk orange
⊠	947		330	orange
=	970		316	lt orange

* Use 2 strands of floss.

The design was stitched on a 10½" x 3½" piece of Vinyl-Weave® (14 ct). Three strands of floss were used for Cross Stitch and 1 for Backstitch (except where indicated in color key). It was inserted in a black mug.

Place design on vinyl 1" from desired short edge and ⅜" from bottom edge; extend green borders to short edges. Place vinyl in mug with short edges aligned with handle. Hand wash mug to protect stitchery.

Design by Ann Townsend.

BEWITCHING SWEATSHIRTS

The little ones in your family will love wearing these sweatshirts when they go a'haunting in the chilly night — and you'll want one too, to bewitch the callers who knock on your door for treats.

Each design was stitched over a 9" square of 8.5 mesh waste canvas on a sweatshirt. Six strands of floss were used for Cross Stitch and 2 for Backstitch. See Working on Waste Canvas, page 143.

Designs by Terrie Lee Steinmeyer.

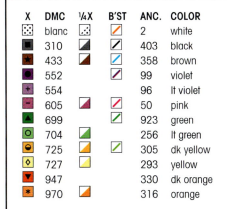

X	DMC	¼X	B'ST	ANC.	COLOR
⊡	blanc	⊡	◨	2	white
■	310	◨	◨	403	black
★	433	◨	◨	358	brown
●	552		◨	99	violet
✚	554			96	lt violet
▬	605	◨	◨	50	pink
▲	699		◨	923	green
○	704	◨		256	lt green
⊖	725		◨	305	dk yellow
◇	727			293	yellow
▼	947			330	dk orange
✱	970	◨		316	orange

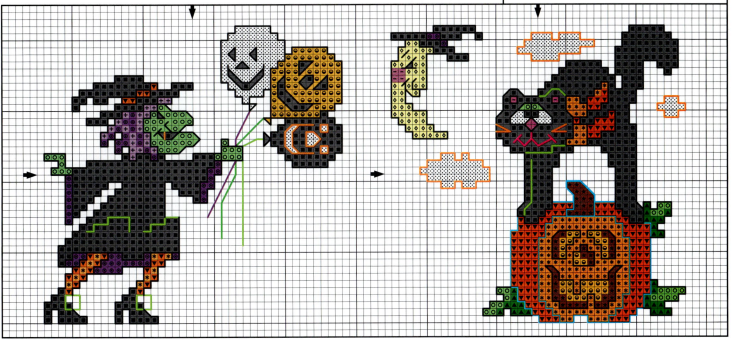

These cute Halloween characters will scare up lots of smiles from your favorite goblins when you stitch the designs on mugs, bread cloths, and tiny tote bags. They're great for serving a steamy witch's brew and sweet treats!

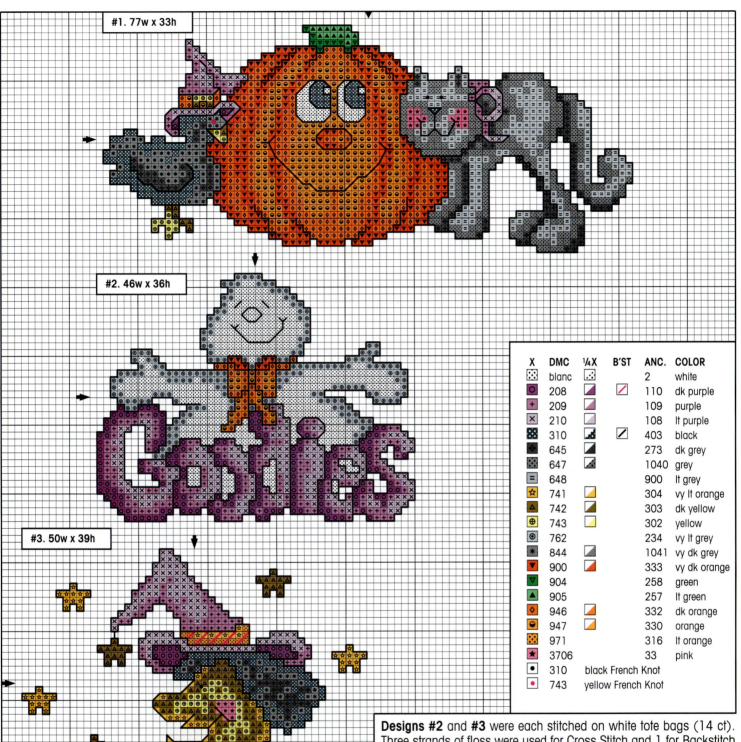

#1. 77w x 33h

#2. 46w x 36h

#3. 50w x 39h

X	DMC	¼X	B'ST	ANC.	COLOR
⊠	blanc	⊡		2	white
⦿	208	◣	◪	110	dk purple
+	209	◣		109	purple
✕	210	◣		108	lt purple
⊠	310	◣	◪	403	black
◆	645	◣		273	dk grey
⊠	647	◣		1040	grey
=	648			900	lt grey
☆	741	◺		304	vy lt orange
▲	742	◺		303	dk yellow
⊕	743	◺		302	yellow
◎	762			234	vy lt grey
✳	844	◣		1041	vy dk grey
▼	900	◪		333	vy dk orange
▽	904			258	green
▲	905			257	lt green
◈	946	◺		332	dk orange
⊖	947	◺		330	orange
⊠	971			316	lt orange
★	3706			33	pink
•	310				black French Knot
•	743				yellow French Knot

Designs #2 and **#3** were each stitched on white tote bags (14 ct). Three strands of floss were used for Cross Stitch and 1 for Backstitch and French Knots.

Design #3 was stitched (omitting quarter stitches) on a 10½" x 3½" piece of Vinyl-Weave® (14 ct). Three strands of floss were used for Cross Stitch and 1 for Backstitch and French Knot. It was inserted in a black mug.

For design placement, center design on right half of vinyl if mug is to be used by a right-handed person or on the left half for a left-handed person. Hand wash mug to protect stitchery.

Designs by Pat Olson.
Needlework adaptation by Christine Street.

Design #1 was stitched on a white bread cover (14 ct). Three strands of floss were used for Cross Stitch and 1 for Backstitch and French Knots. The design was centered horizontally with bottom of design ½" from beginning of fringe.

Framed and tucked inside a grapevine wreath, this trio of happy pumpkins will add a whimsical touch to your celebration.

The design was stitched on a 9" x 6" piece of White Aida (14 ct). Three strands of floss were used for Cross Stitch and 1 for Backstitch. It was inserted in a purchased frame (5" x 2¾" opening) and attached to an 8" dia. grapevine wreath.

Refer to photo to hot glue framed piece to grapevine wreath. Glue plastic spiders to frame as desired. Cut 1 yard lengths of assorted sizes and colors of ribbons. Tie ribbons into a bow. Glue bow to frame. Arrange ribbons as desired and glue to wreath and frame. Trim ends of ribbons as needed.

Design by Terrie Lee Steinmeyer© 1994.

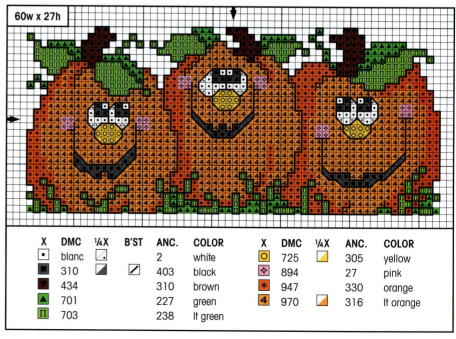

60w x 27h

X	DMC	¼X	B'ST	ANC.	COLOR	X	DMC	¼X	ANC.	COLOR
•	blanc	⬚		2	white	O	725	◨	305	yellow
■	310	◣	╱	403	black	◆	894		27	pink
■	434			310	brown	✳	947		330	orange
▲	701			227	green	4	970	◨	316	lt orange
Ⅱ	703			238	lt green					

88

With this spellbinding alphabet, you can conjure up lots of holiday fun! We stitched the words "Boo Bag" on a mini tote that's big on style.

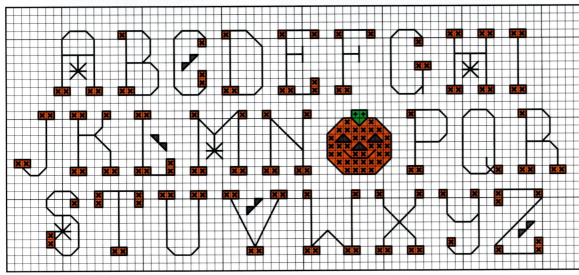

X	DMC	1/4X	B'ST	COLOR
	310			black
✖	608			orange
✦	910			green

BOO BAG was stitched over 2 fabric threads on an Ivory Lil' Tote (14 ct). Six strands of floss were used for Cross Stitch and 2 for Backstitch.

Dressed in a skeleton suit, this gentle bear proves that he's all heart. He looks absolutely adorable stitched on a sweatshirt!

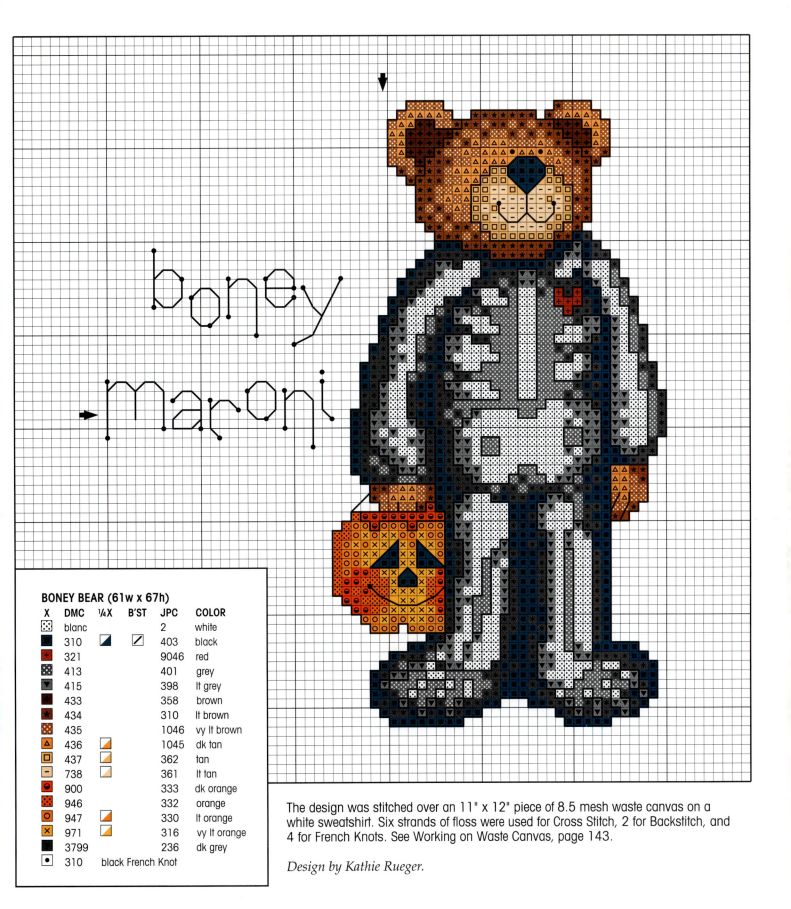

BONEY BEAR (61w x 67h)

X	DMC	¼X	B'ST	JPC	COLOR
⬚	blanc			2	white
◼	310	◣	╱	403	black
✚	321			9046	red
▦	413			401	grey
▼	415			398	lt grey
◼	433			358	brown
★	434			310	lt brown
▨	435			1046	vy lt brown
△	436	◤		1045	dk tan
▢	437	◤		362	tan
–	738	◤		361	lt tan
⦿	900			333	dk orange
▨	946			332	orange
⊙	947	◤		330	lt orange
✕	971	◤		316	vy lt orange
◼	3799			236	dk grey
⦿	310				black French Knot

The design was stitched over an 11" x 12" piece of 8.5 mesh waste canvas on a white sweatshirt. Six strands of floss were used for Cross Stitch, 2 for Backstitch, and 4 for French Knots. See Working on Waste Canvas, page 143.

Design by Kathie Rueger.

THANKSGIVING

*T*he very mention of Thanksgiving calls up memories of cozy kitchens filled with good things to eat. Aside from the abundance of food, the day is customarily a time for reflecting upon our many blessings. Prayers of thanksgiving are offered, and friends and family celebrate the day. This keepsake collection of designs — from the seasonal sampler shown here to a bounty of table linens — will enrich your festivities for years to come.

75w x 103h

The design was stitched over two fabric threads on a 14" x 16" piece of Tea-Dyed Irish Linen (28 ct). Three strands of floss were used for Cross Stitch and 1 for Backstitch. It was custom framed.

Design by Polly Carbonari.

X	DMC	ANC.	X	DMC	B'ST	ANC.
355	1014		890		218
356	5975		924		851
367	217		926		850
729	890		3750		1036

THANKSGIVING TOPPER

Dressed up like a turkey, this heart-warming bear is eager to express his thankfulness. He looks especially sweet topping a jar of seasonal candy.

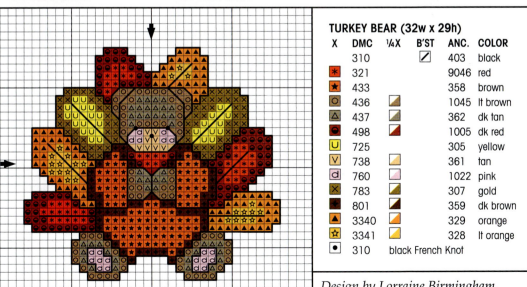

TURKEY BEAR (32w x 29h)

X	DMC	¼X	B'ST	ANC.	COLOR
	310		╱	403	black
✳	321			9046	red
★	433			358	brown
○	436	▨		1045	lt brown
▲	437			362	dk tan
●	498	▨		1005	dk red
U	725			305	yellow
V	738	▨		361	tan
d	760	▨		1022	pink
✕	783	▨		307	gold
■	801	▨		359	dk brown
▲	3340	▨		329	orange
☆	3341	▨		328	lt orange
●	310				black French Knot

The design was stitched on a 6" square of Ivory Aida (14 ct). Three strands of floss were used for Cross Stitch and 1 strand for Backstitch and French Knots. It was inserted in wide-mouth jar lid.

For jar lid, use outer edge of jar lid for pattern and cut a circle from adhesive mounting board. Using opening of jar lid for pattern, cut a circle of batting. Center batting on adhesive side of board and press into place. Center stitched piece on batting and press edges onto adhesive board; trim edges close to board. Glue board inside jar lid. (**Note:** Mason jar puff-up kit may be used to finish jar lid.)

Design by Lorraine Birmingham.

95

The beauty of autumn leaves is captured in these five designs for fingertip towels. Displayed in the kitchen or bath, the delicate set serves as a reminder of the many blessings of fall.

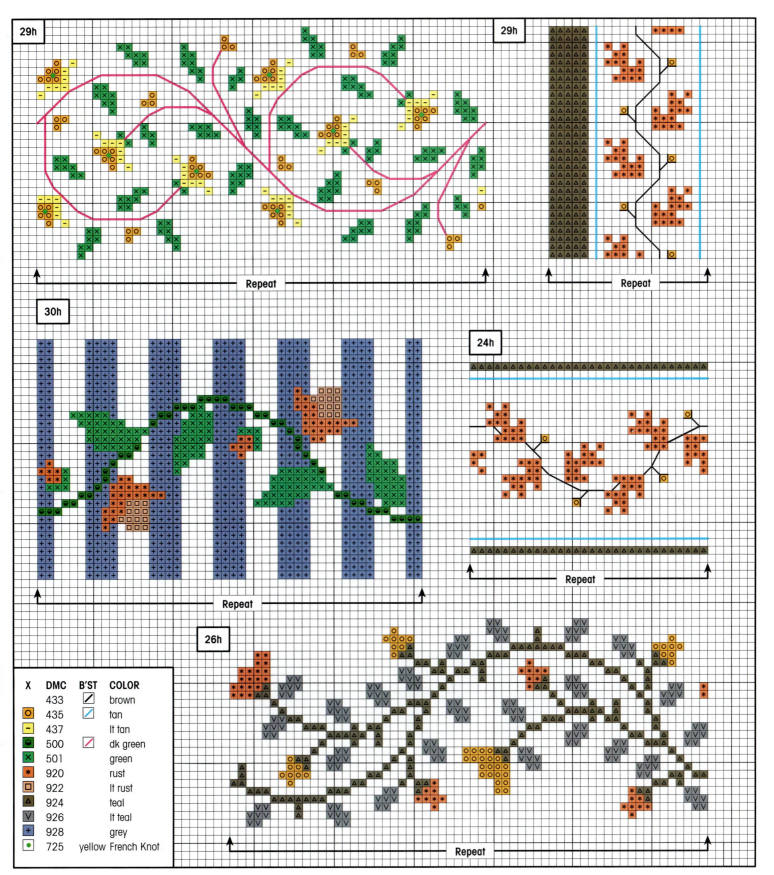

Each design was stitched on the 14 ct insert of an ecru fingertip towel. Three strands of floss were used for Cross Stitch and 1 for Backstitch and French Knots.

Designs by Jane Chandler.

X	DMC	B'ST	COLOR
	433	/	brown
O	435	/	tan
-	437		lt tan
◉	500	/	dk green
X	501		green
*	920		rust
□	922		lt rust
△	924		teal
V	926		lt teal
+	928		grey
●	725		yellow French Knot

Perfect for wearing during the Thanksgiving holidays, this embellished sweater features Peter Pilgrim and his pet turkey, Trot. The pair is worked directly over the knit stitches of the sweater.

I LOVE TURKEY (51w x 82h)

X	DMC	JPC	COLOR
⊡	blanc	1001	white
■	310	8403	black
◇	353	3006	pink
O	742	2303	yellow
−	754	2331	peach
★	762	8510	grey
■	839	5360	dk brown
C	840	5379	brown
✕	841	5376	lt brown
□	842	5933	vy lt brown
✱	920	3337	orange
+	931	7051	blue
S	3750		dk blue

This design may be worked in Cross Stitch on any sweater knit in stockinette, a stitch which forms rows of stitches shaped like "V's." The number of stitches and rows per inch, commonly referred to as gauge, will vary from sweater to sweater. A medium gauge, approximately 7-9 stitches per inch and 9-11 rows per inch, is best for working Cross Stitch on a sweater. The number of strands of floss to use will vary with the gauge of the sweater. For this project, 6 strands of embroidery floss were used on a sweater with a gauge of 8 stitches per inch and 10 rows per inch. It may be necessary to experiment with a few stitches on a sweater of a different gauge.

STITCH DIAGRAM

Counted Cross Stitch (X): Work one Cross Stitch to correspond to each colored square on the chart. Referring to **Fig. 1**, bring threaded needle up at 1; insert needle at 2. Bring needle up again at 3; insert needle at 4. Always insert needle between strands of yarn. Keep stitching tension consistent with tension of knit fabric.

Fig. 1

The design was cross stitched on a purchased sweater with top edge of design 1½" from the bottom of neckband. Six strands of floss were used for Cross Stitch. Referring to photo for placement, tack a 4" length of ⅛"w ribbon to turkey's neck and Pilgrim's hand. Tie a 5" length of ribbon in a bow; trim ends and tack bow to turkey's neck.

Design by Karen Wood.

Thanksgiving feasts traditionally include baskets filled with hot, fresh-baked bread — and that calls for special serving linens. These pretty cloths celebrate the bounty of the season.

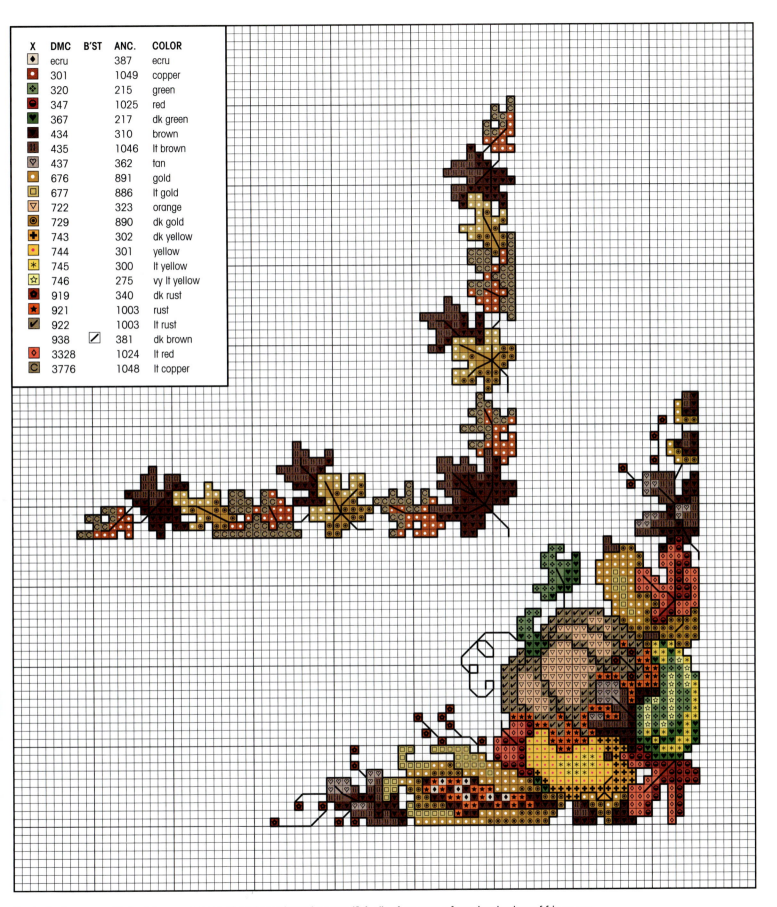

X	DMC	B'ST	ANC.	COLOR
♦	ecru		387	ecru
▣	301		1049	copper
✿	320		215	green
◓	347		1025	red
▼	367		217	dk green
▬	434		310	brown
Ⅲ	435		1046	lt brown
♡	437		362	tan
⬗	676		891	gold
▢	677		886	lt gold
▽	722		323	orange
⊙	729		890	dk gold
✚	743		302	dk yellow
⦁	744		301	yellow
✳	745		300	lt yellow
☆	746		275	vy lt yellow
⬠	919		340	dk rust
★	921		1003	rust
✓	922		1003	lt rust
	938	╱	381	dk brown
◆	3328		1024	lt red
C	3776		1048	lt copper

Each design was stitched in one corner of an ivory bread cover (14 ct), 4 squares from beginning of fringe on each side. Three strands of floss were used for Cross Stitch and 1 for Backstitch.

Designs by Deborah Lambein.

TURKEY DAY TOWEL

Bears and bunnies portray American Colonists and native Indians from the first Thanksgiving on this cute fingertip towel. It's sure to add a bit of fun to turkey day!

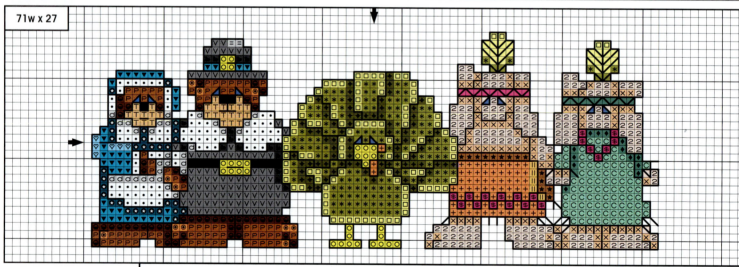

71w x 27

The design was stitched on the 14 ct insert of a white fingertip towel. Three strands of floss were used for Cross Stitch and 1 for Backstitch.

Design by Karen Wood.

X	DMC	¾X	B'ST	ANC.	COLOR	X	DMC	¼X	¾X	ANC.	COLOR	X	DMC	ANC.	COLOR
•	blanc			2	white	✦	610			889	dk taupe	d	762	234	vy lt grey
■	310	◣	╱	403	black	✳	611		╱	898	taupe	★	797	132	dk blue
V	317			400	grey	▫	612			832	lt taupe	▼	798	131	blue
≡	318			399	lt grey	▪	720			326	dk orange	♡	799	136	lt blue
▨	413			401	dk grey	+	721			324	orange	$	917	89	plum
▩	433			358	dk brown	‖	722			323	lt orange	◆	958	187	dk aqua
P	434	◢		310	brown	O	725			305	yellow	C	959	186	aqua
◉	435			1046	lt brown	✕	738			361	tan				
T	437			362	dk tan	2	739		▫	387	lt tan				

102

"Give Thanks" and "Peace and Plenty" are sentiments of the season that merit sharing. You can make the designs into ornaments like ours, or create a cornucopia of projects.

Each design was stitched on a 4" square of Antique White Aida (18 ct). Two strands of floss were used for Cross Stitch and 1 for Backstitch. They were inserted in round frames (2½" dia. opening).

Designs by Holly DeFount.

X	DMC	¼X	B'ST	ANC.	COLOR
•	blanc			2	white
✦	319	◩	◤	218	dk green
★	349			13	red
✳	350			11	lt red
⊙	367	◩		217	green
■	498			1005	dk red
☆	722	◩		323	orange
△	729			890	gold
+	744			301	yellow
▲	817			13	dk red
	838		◤	380	brown
◼	840			379	dk taupe
×	841			378	taupe
▽	842			388	lt taupe
⊜	989			242	green

Displayed on a wreath, this welcoming design invites family and friends to share in a day of good food and thanksgiving.

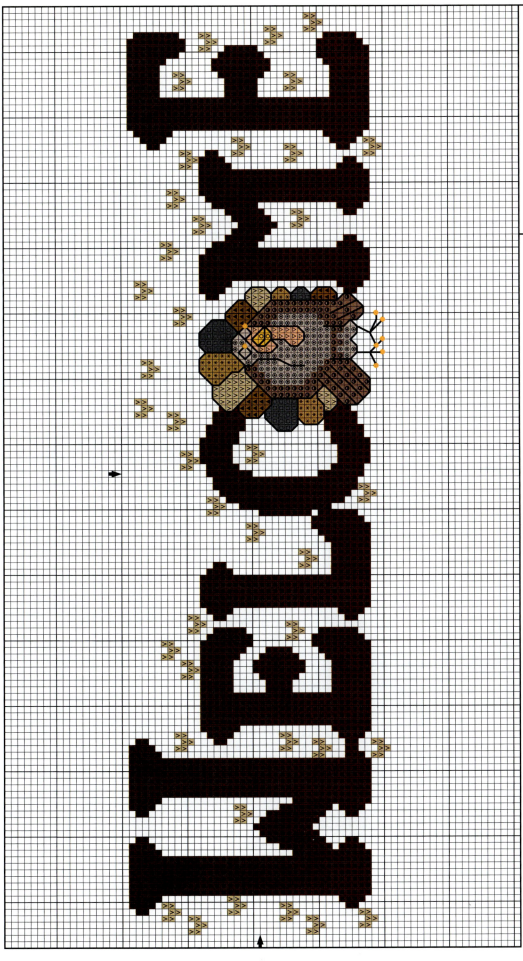

TURKEY WELCOME (141w x 40h)

X	¼X	B'ST	DMC	ANC.	COLOR
			433	358	brown
			434	310	lt brown
			437	362	dk tan
			744	301	yellow
			817	13	lt red
			919	340	vy dk rust
			920	1004	dk rust
			921	1003	rust
			922	1003	lt rust
			3371	382	brown black
		◻	3371		brown black French Knot

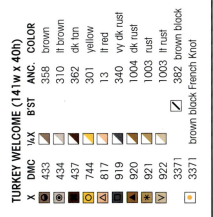

The design was stitched on a 9⁷⁄₈" x 4¹⁄₄" piece of Ivory Aida (18 ct). Two strands of floss were used for Cross Stitch and 1 for Backstitch and French Knots. It was made into a pillow and attached to a grapevine wreath.

For pillow, cut backing fabric (same fabric as stitched piece) same size as the stitched piece. Matching wrong sides, use 2 strands of floss to work running stitch (over and under 2 fabric threads) ¹⁄₂" from top and bottom edges and one side edge. Stuff pillow with polyester fiberfill. Continue working running stitches across remaining side of pillow ¹⁄₂" from edge. Fringe fabric to one square from running stitches.

Design by Kathie Rueger.

For generations, Thanksgiving in America has meant gathering with friends and relatives to break bread. These autumn-inspired bread covers are a nice addition to your holiday table.

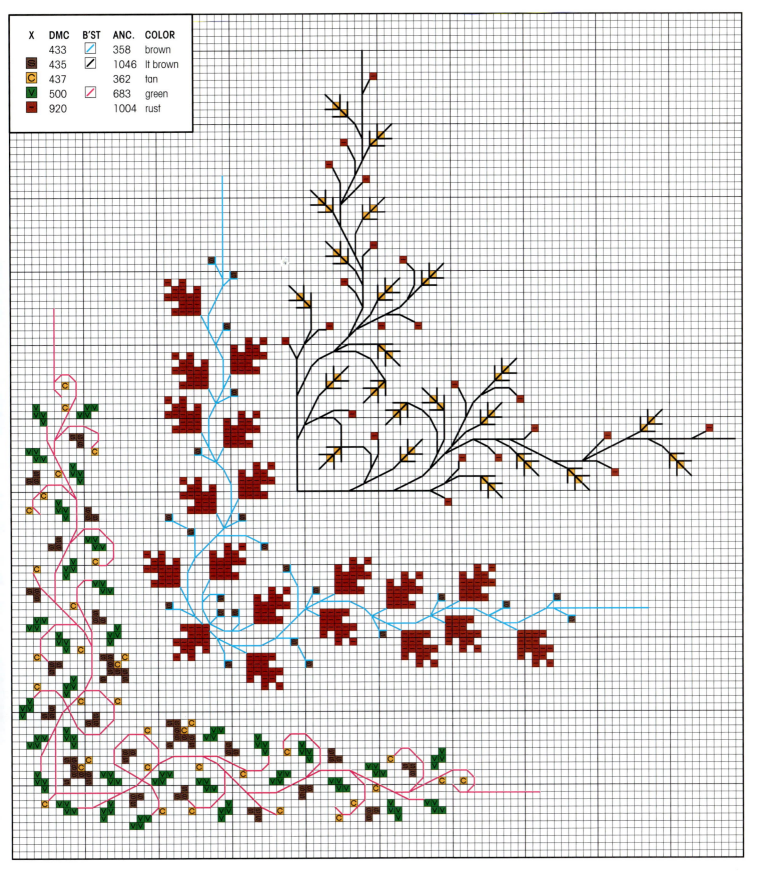

X	DMC	B'ST	ANC.	COLOR
	433		358	brown
S	435		1046	lt brown
C	437		362	tan
V	500		683	green
	920		1004	rust

Each design was stitched on an ivory bread cover (14 ct) ½" from the beginning of fringe. Three strands of floss were used for Cross Stitch and 1 strand for Backstitch. The Backstitch border was extended around the edges of each bread cover.

Designs by Jane Chandler.

CHRISTMAS

*C*hristmas is our favorite time of the year!
We've gathered a collection of quick-to-stitch
projects that will make this your merriest holiday
ever. You'll find some fun finishes for clothing,
as well as more traditional decorations, such as
these ornaments and our poinsettia bread cloths.
These projects make wonderful gifts for friends
and family — and for yourself!

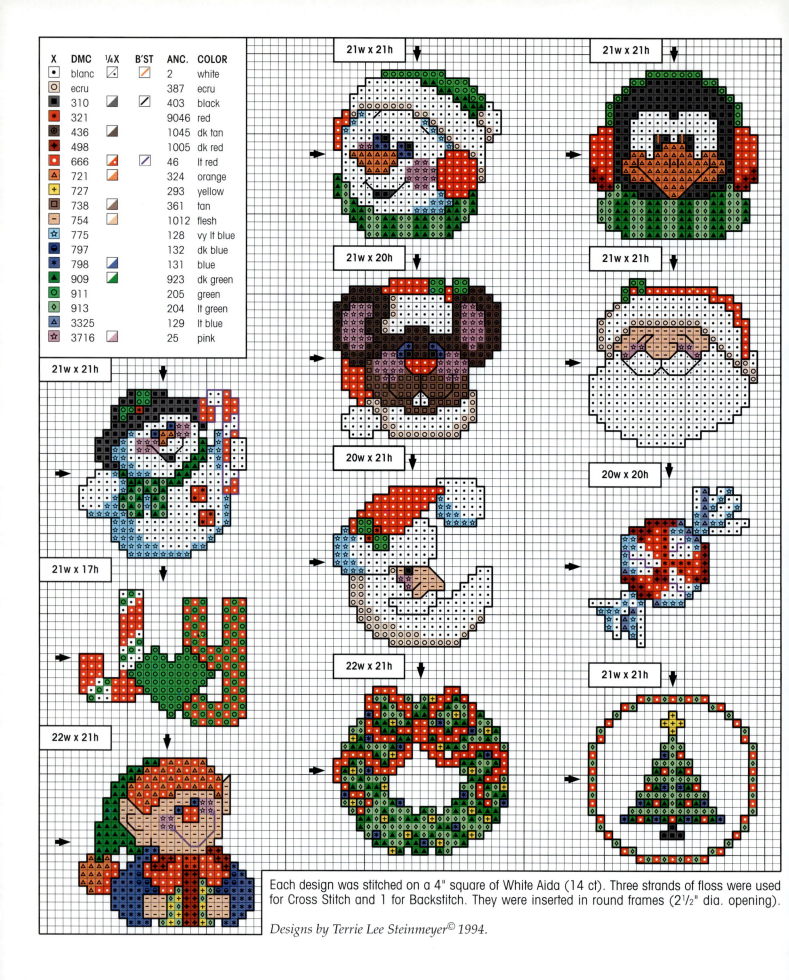

Each design was stitched on a 4" square of White Aida (14 ct). Three strands of floss were used for Cross Stitch and 1 for Backstitch. They were inserted in round frames (2½" dia. opening).

Designs by Terrie Lee Steinmeyer© 1994.

NUTCRACKER PARADE

These quaint nutcracker ornaments will bring a timeless look to your Christmas tree. Stiffened and completed with ribbon hangers, the dandy characters will also make treasured holiday keepsakes for anyone on your gift list.

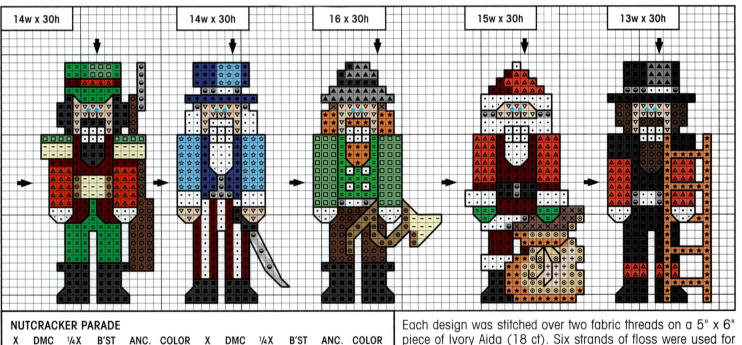

| 14w x 30h | 14w x 30h | 16 x 30h | 15w x 30h | 13w x 30h |

NUTCRACKER PARADE

X	DMC	¼X	B'ST	ANC.	COLOR	X	DMC	¼X	B'ST	ANC.	COLOR
●	blanc			2	white	⊕	676			891	gold
▲	309			42	lt red	−	677			886	lt gold
■	310		◪	403	black	◉	738			361	tan
✳	334			977	blue	+	739			387	lt tan
◎	434			310	brown	⊖	762			234	lt grey
✕	435			1046	lt brown	▽	948			1011	peach
★	437			362	dk tan	▲	3799			236	grey
⬟	498			1005	red	☆	3325			129	lt blue
═	562			210	green	●	310			black French Knot
□	563			208	lt green						

Each design was stitched over two fabric threads on a 5" x 6" piece of Ivory Aida (18 ct). Six strands of floss were used for Cross Stitch and 2 for Backstitch and French Knots. They were stiffened and made into ornaments.

For each ornament, cut one piece of medium-weight fabric same size as the stitched piece for backing. Apply a heavy coat of fabric stiffener to the back of stitched piece using a small foam brush. Matching wrong sides, place stitched piece on backing fabric, smoothing stitched piece while pressing fabrics together; allow to dry. Apply stiffener to backing fabric; allow to dry. Referring to photo, trim stitched piece close to design. Fold a 4" length of ⅛"w ribbon in half and glue to back of ornament.

Designs by Deborah Lambein.

You'll love sporting our "Santa Claus University" sweatshirt! Embellished with a profile of the jolly old gent, it'll lend a lighthearted touch to your holiday wardrobe.

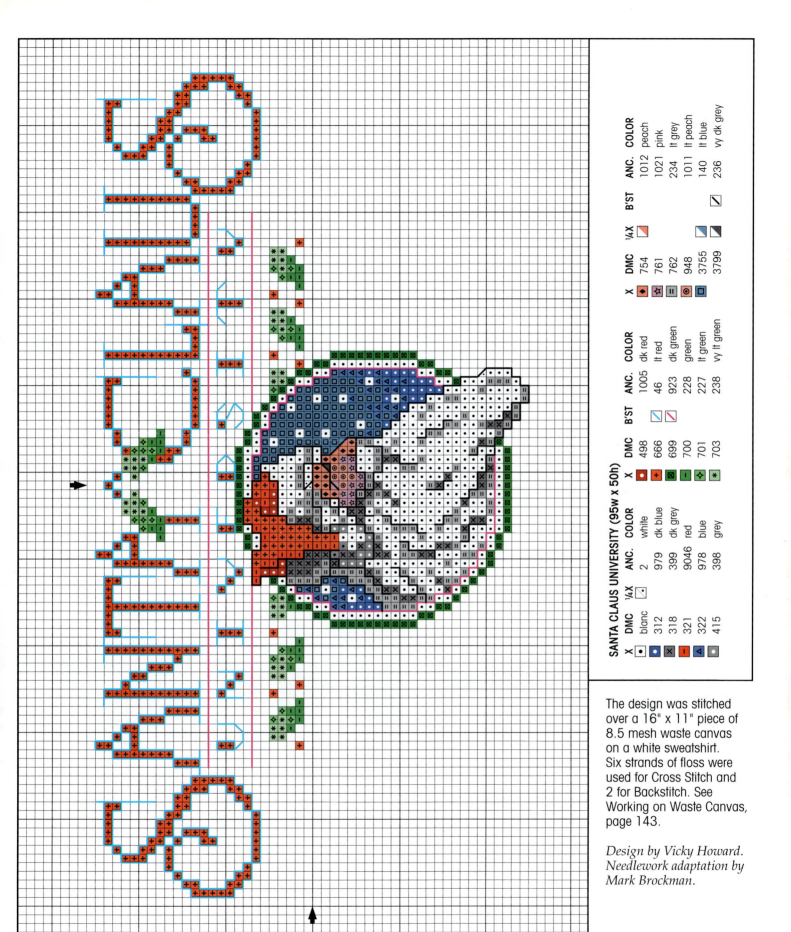

SANTA CLAUS UNIVERSITY (95w x 50h)

X	DMC	ANC.	COLOR		¼X		B'ST		X	DMC	ANC.	COLOR
•	blanc	2	white		⊡				●	754	1012	peach
◉	312	979	dk blue						✶	761	1021	pink
✕	318	399	dk grey						‖	762	234	lt grey
I	321	9046	red						◉	948	1011	lt peach
◁	322	978	blue						▣	3755	140	lt blue
⊙	415	398	grey							3799	236	vy dk grey

X	DMC	ANC.	COLOR		B'ST		X	DMC	ANC.	COLOR
●	498	1005	dk red				I	700	228	green
+	666	46	lt red				◆	701	227	lt green
⊠	699	923	dk green				✱	703	238	vy lt green

The design was stitched over a 16" x 11" piece of 8.5 mesh waste canvas on a white sweatshirt. Six strands of floss were used for Cross Stitch and 2 for Backstitch. See Working on Waste Canvas, page 143.

Design by Vicky Howard. Needlework adaptation by Mark Brockman.

Herald the season with these heart-shaped ornaments featuring angelic music makers. Satiny cording and tassels provide an extra touch of elegance.

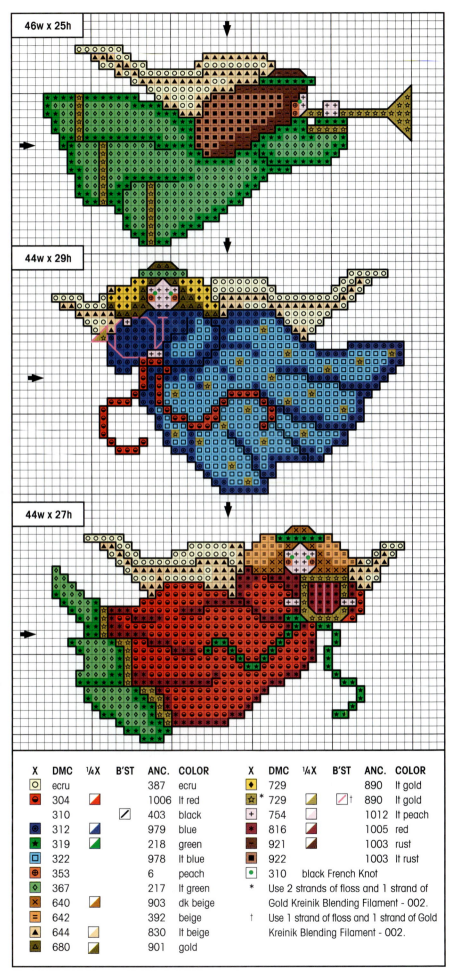

Each **Angel** was stitched on an 8" x 6" piece of Dirty Aida (14 ct). Three strands of floss were used for Cross Stitch and 1 for all other stitches, unless indicated otherwise in color key. They were made into heart ornaments.

For each ornament you will need tracing paper, 8" x 6" piece of Dirty Aida for backing, 10" x 5" piece of adhesive board, 10" x 5" piece of batting, 12" length of ¼" dia. cording with attached seam allowance, 2¼" fringe tassel, embroidery floss for hanger, and craft glue.

For each heart pattern, fold tracing paper in half and place fold on dashed line of pattern; trace and cut out traced pattern. Draw around Small Heart pattern twice on adhesive board and twice on batting; cut out. Remove paper from adhesive board and adhere one batting piece to each adhesive board piece. Center Large Heart pattern over stitched piece; draw around pattern. Cut out stitched piece. Cut backing fabric the same size as stitched piece.

For ornament front, clip ³⁄₈" into edges of stitched piece at ½" intervals. Center stitched piece over batting side of one adhesive board piece; fold edges to wrong side and glue in place. Repeat with backing fabric and remaining adhesive board piece for ornament back.

Glue cording seam allowance to wrong side of ornament front, beginning at top point of heart. Glue tassel to wrong side of ornament front at bottom of heart.

For hanger, cut two 30" lengths of embroidery floss. Fold floss lengths in half and knot all ends together. Holding knot with one hand, insert one finger of other hand through loop of floss and twist until tight on finger. Holding floss so that it will not untwist, remove finger. Fold floss in half, matching the knot to the loop; knot them together. Holding knot with one hand, use other hand to stretch and slowly release floss to make a smooth cord. Glue ends of cord to the wrong side of ornament front at top of heart. Glue wrong sides of ornament front and back together. Weight with a heavy book until glue is dry.

Designs by Lorraine Birmingham.

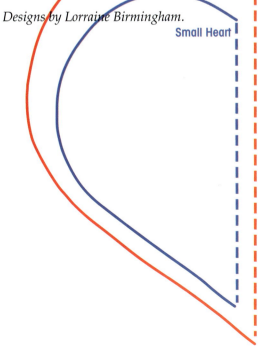

X	DMC	¼X	B'ST	ANC.	COLOR
○	ecru			387	ecru
▨	304	◹		1006	lt red
	310		◿	403	black
◉	312	◥		979	blue
★	319	◥		218	green
▣	322			978	lt blue
⊕	353			6	peach
◈	367			217	lt green
✕	640	◹		903	dk beige
=	642			392	beige
▲	644	◿		830	lt beige
◮	680			901	gold

X	DMC	¼X	B'ST	ANC.	COLOR
◆	729			890	lt gold
☆	* 729	◹	◿ †	890	lt gold
+	754			1012	lt peach
✳	816			1005	red
▬	921		◿	1003	rust
■	922			1003	lt rust
⊙	310				black French Knot
*					Use 2 strands of floss and 1 strand of Gold Kreinik Blending Filament - 002.
†					Use 1 strand of floss and 1 strand of Gold Kreinik Blending Filament - 002.

115

Our festive fingertip towels will make nice gifts for friends who enjoy decorating for Christmas as much as you do. Featuring pretty poinsettias, each design will lend traditional appeal to the bath or kitchen.

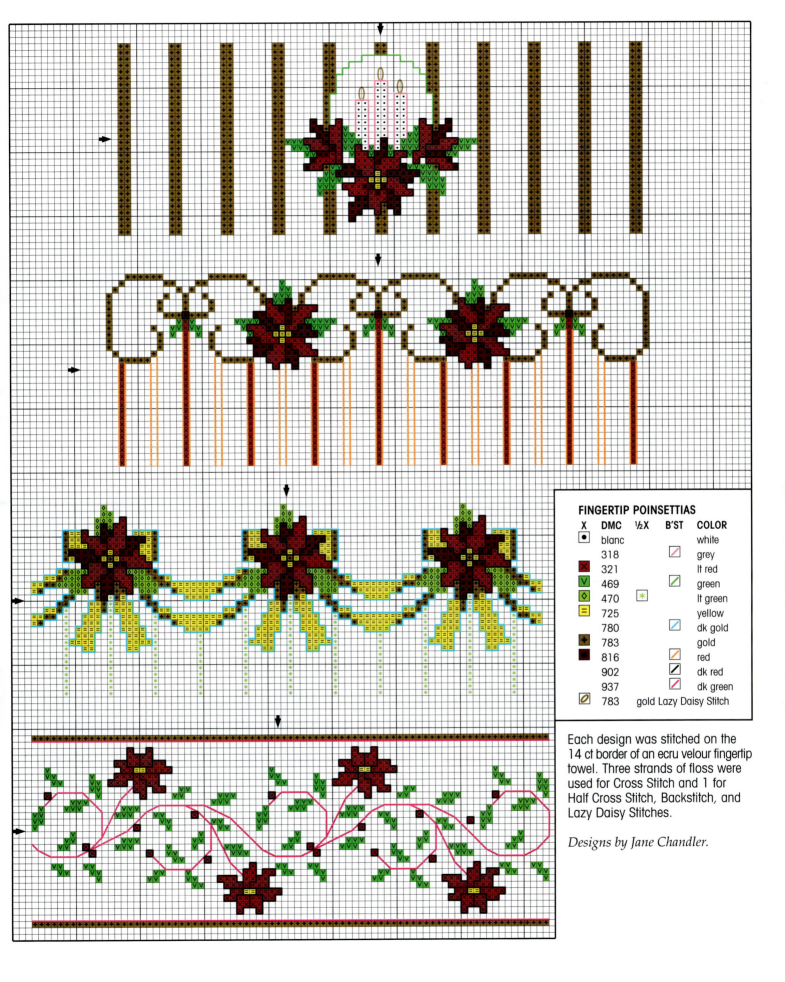

FINGERTIP POINSETTIAS

X	DMC	½X	B'ST	COLOR
●	blanc			white
	318		/	grey
×	321			lt red
V	469		/	green
◊	470	*		lt green
=	725			yellow
	780		/	dk gold
◆	783			gold
■	816		/	red
	902		/	dk red
	937		/	dk green
⬦	783			gold Lazy Daisy Stitch

Each design was stitched on the 14 ct border of an ecru velour fingertip towel. Three strands of floss were used for Cross Stitch and 1 for Half Cross Stitch, Backstitch, and Lazy Daisy Stitches.

Designs by Jane Chandler.

117

These mini pillow ornaments will add North Woods charm to your Yuletide decorating. You can use all ten together to give your tree a homespun touch, or give them individually as thoughtful little gifts.

RUSTIC TREE TRIMS

X	DMC	¼X	B'ST	ANC.	COLOR
•	blanc			2	white
■	310			403	black
+	321		/	9046	red
	433			358	brown
	434			310	lt brown
	436			1045	tan
×	562	◣		210	green
	738	◺		361	lt tan
–	744			301	yellow
	3731			76	pink
•	310		black French Knot		

Each design was stitched on an 8" x 7" piece of Fiddler's Cloth (14 ct). Three strands of floss were used for Cross Stitch and 1 for Backstitch and French Knots. They were made into mini pillow ornaments.

For each mini pillow ornament, trim stitched piece ¾" larger than design on all sides. Cut a piece of Fiddler's Cloth the same size as stitched piece for backing. With wrong sides facing, use 2 strands of red floss and a running stitch to join fabric pieces together 4 squares from sides and bottom of design. Stuff with polyester fiberfill. Repeat to stitch across top of ornament. Fringe fabric to within 1 square of running stitch. For hanger, cut a 6" length of ⅛"w ribbon and blind stitch to back of ornament.

Designs by Polly Carbonari.

Santa and his jolly pals celebrate the spirit of the holidays in these three whimsical scenes. The designs are perfect for making merry mugs or embellishing children's clothing.

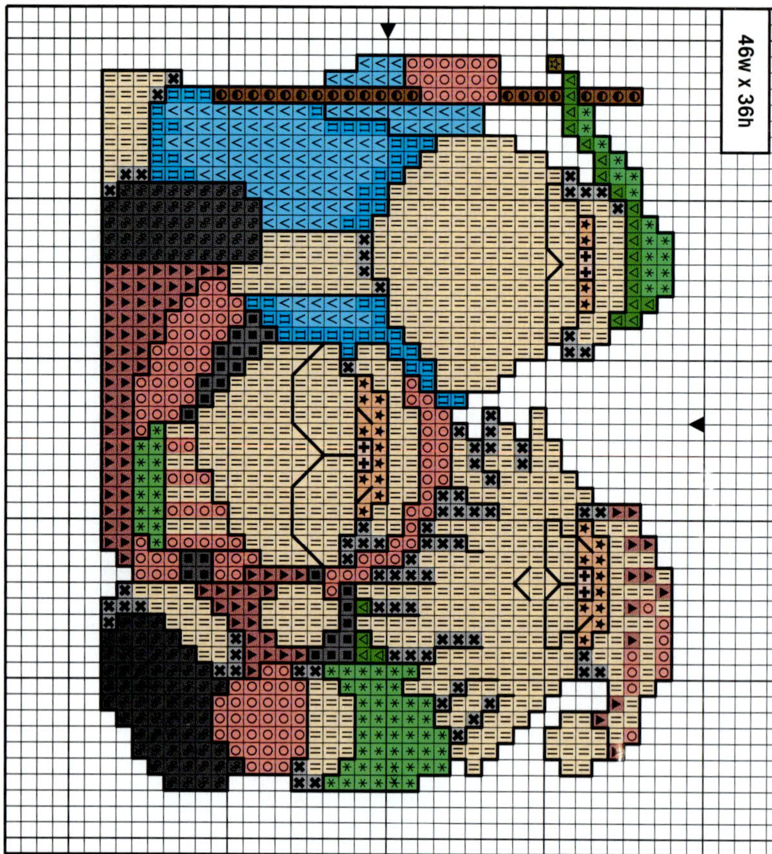

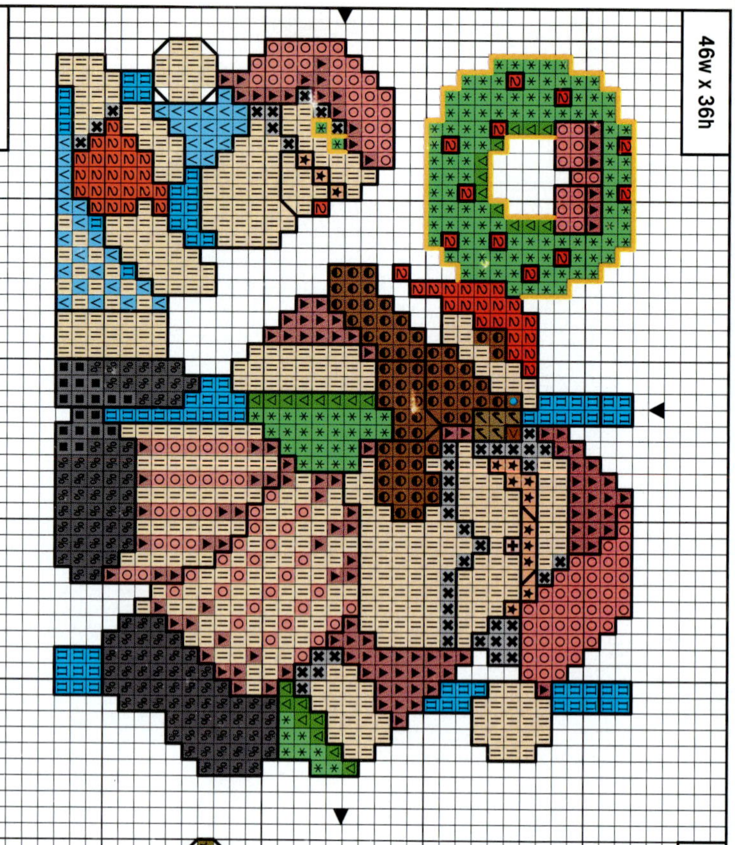

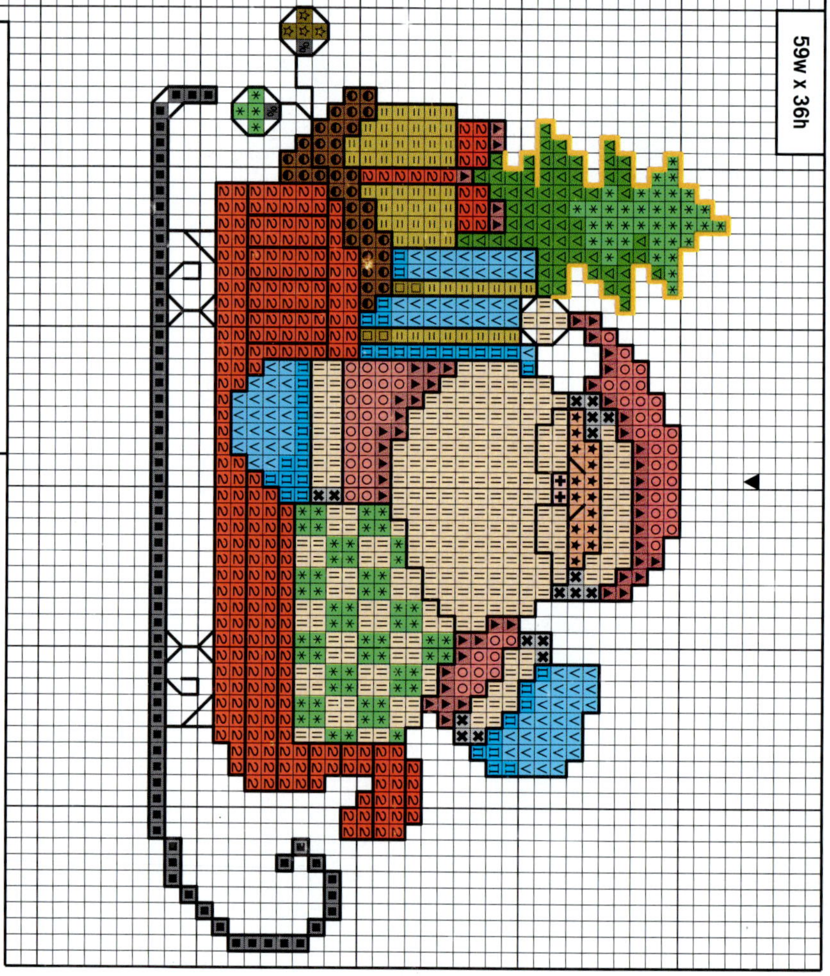

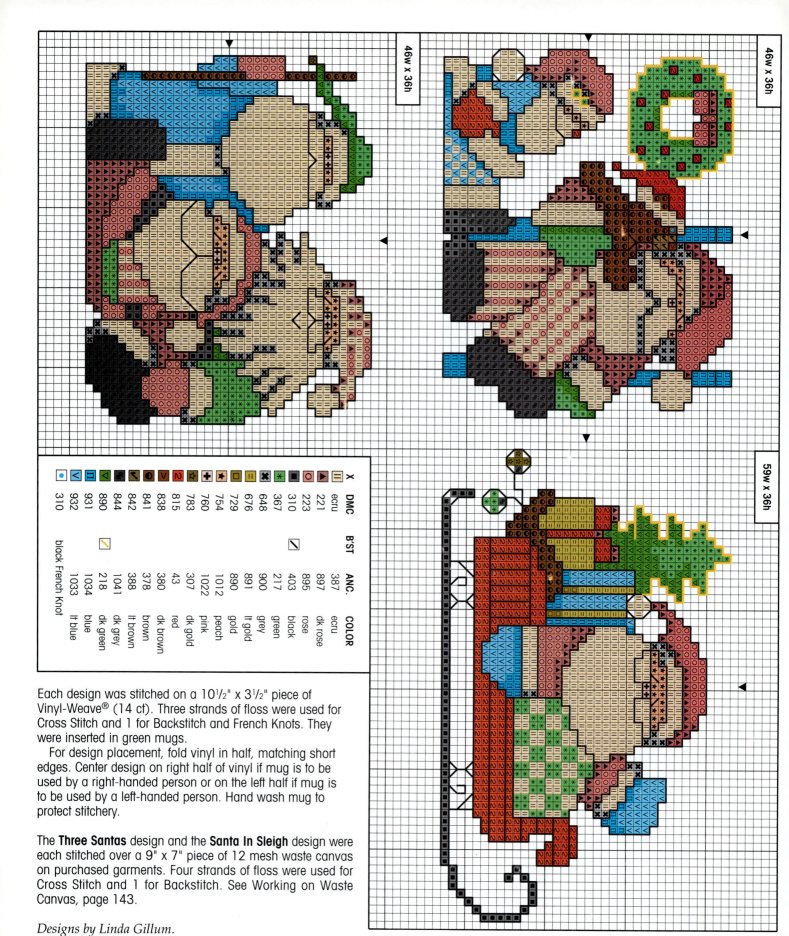

X	DMC	B'ST	ANC.	COLOR
	ecru		387	ecru
	221		897	dk rose
	223		895	rose
	310	✓	403	black
	367		217	green
	648		900	grey
	676		891	lt gold
	729		890	gold
	754		1012	peach
	760		1022	pink
	783		307	dk gold
	815		43	red
	838		380	dk brown
	841		378	brown
	842		388	lt brown
	844		1041	dk grey
	890	✓	218	dk green
	931		1034	blue
	932		1033	lt blue
	310	black French Knot		

Each design was stitched on a 10½" x 3½" piece of Vinyl-Weave® (14 ct). Three strands of floss were used for Cross Stitch and 1 for Backstitch and French Knots. They were inserted in green mugs.

For design placement, fold vinyl in half, matching short edges. Center design on right half of vinyl if mug is to be used by a right-handed person or on the left half if mug is to be used by a left-handed person. Hand wash mug to protect stitchery.

The **Three Santas** design and the **Santa In Sleigh** design were each stitched over a 9" x 7" piece of 12 mesh waste canvas on purchased garments. Four strands of floss were used for Cross Stitch and 1 for Backstitch. See Working on Waste Canvas, page 143.

Designs by Linda Gillum.

Accented with tiny glass beads, a trio of snowflakes adorns our colorful jar toppers. With these quick and easy designs, you'll be able to add a frosty touch to all your holiday treats.

FROSTY TOPS (21w x 21h)

X	DMC	ANC.	COLOR
■	blanc	2	white
●	Mill Hill Bead #00479		

Designs by Kandace Thomas.

Note: Each design was stitched over 2 fabric threads on a 5" square of fabric. Three strands of floss were used for Cross Stitch and 1 for attaching beads. They were inserted in small-mouth jar lids. See Attaching Beads, page 143.

Design #1 was stitched on Victorian Christmas Green Lugana (25 ct).
Design #2 was stitched on Raspberry Lugana (25 ct).
Design #3 was stitched on Navy Lugana (25 ct).

For jar lid, use outer edge of jar lid for pattern and cut a circle from adhesive mounting board. Using opening of jar lid for pattern, cut a circle of batting. Center batting on adhesive board and press in place. Center stitched piece on batting and press edges onto adhesive board; trim edges close to board. Glue board inside jar lid. (**Note:** Mason jar puff-up kits may be used to finish jar lids.)

Gracefully adorned with six tiny reindeer, our homespun sampler pays tribute to the majestic Christmas tree. The simple charm of this quaint piece is sure to enhance your decor.

O CHRISTMAS TREE (98w x 119h)

X	DMC	ANC.	COLOR	X	DMC	ANC.	COLOR
+	501	878	blue green	▫	934	862	lt green
▽	610	889	brown	=	935	861	green
✳	680	901	gold	◉	936	269	dk green
◆	729	890	lt gold	◉	3031	360	dk brown
⊠	902	897	dk rose	P	3726	1018	rose

The design was stitched over 2 fabric threads on a 13" x 15" piece of Belfast Raw Linen (32 ct). Two strands of floss were used for Cross Stitch. It was custom framed.

Design by Cecilia Turner.

With these quick-to-stitch designs for fingertip towels, it's easy to set a merry mood in the kitchen or bath. The four charming scenes look great just hanging around or tucked into a gift basket for a special friend.

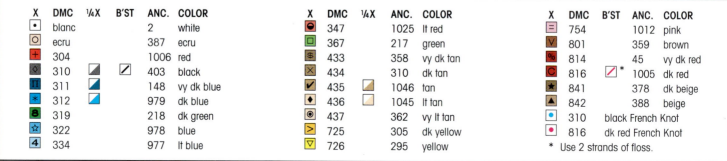

X	DMC	¼X	B'ST	ANC.	COLOR	X	DMC	¼X	ANC.	COLOR	X	DMC	B'ST	ANC.	COLOR
•	blanc			2	white	⊖	347		1025	lt red	⊟	754		1012	pink
○	ecru			387	ecru	□	367		217	green	V	801		359	brown
+	304		◹	1006	red	$	433		358	vy dk tan	%	814		45	vy dk red
◈	310	◹	◹	403	black	✗	434		310	dk tan	C	816	◹*	1005	dk red
⊓	311	◥		148	vy dk blue	✓	435	◹	1046	tan	★	841		378	dk beige
＊	312	◥		979	dk blue	◆	436	◹	1045	lt tan	▲	842		388	beige
❀	319			218	dk green	◉	437		362	vy lt tan	•	310			black French Knot
☆	322			978	blue	>	725		305	dk yellow	•	816			dk red French Knot
4	334			977	lt blue	▽	726		295	yellow		* Use 2 strands of floss.			

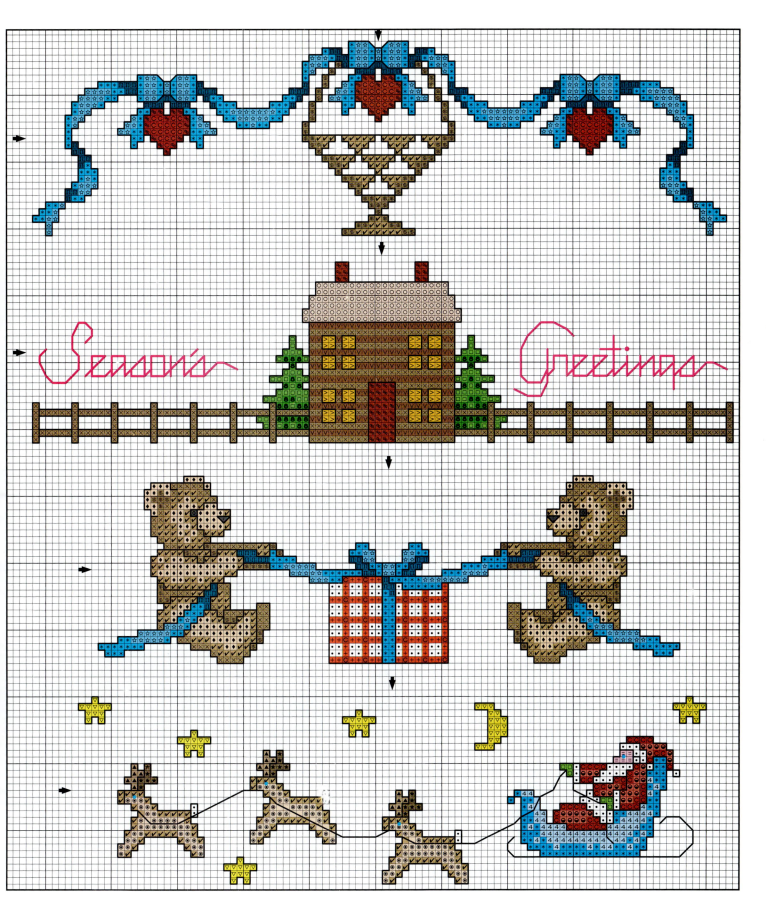

Each design was stitched on the 14 ct border of a velour fingertip towel.
Three strands of floss were used for Cross Stitch and 1 for Backstitch
and French Knots (unless otherwise noted in color key).

Designs by Jane Chandler.

Stitched on perforated paper, our holiday motifs are glued around wooden thread spools to create these splendid tree-trimmers. You'll have fun finishing the miniature ornaments with fabric yo-yos, tassels, and clothespin clips and candles.

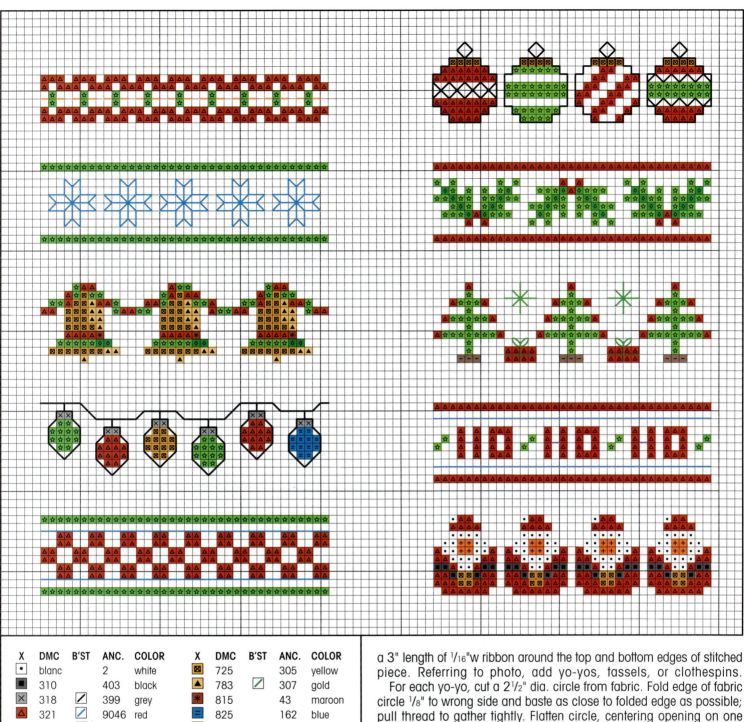

X	DMC	B'ST	ANC.	COLOR		X	DMC	B'ST	ANC.	COLOR
•	blanc		2	white		⊠	725		305	yellow
■	310		403	black		▲	783	▨	307	gold
×	318	╱	399	grey		✳	815		43	maroon
▲	321	╱	9046	red		⊟	825		162	blue
	321	╱ *	9046	red		+	3779		868	peach
−	434		310	brown		⊘	783			gold Lazy Daisy Stitch
◇	699	╱	923	dk green		*				Use 2 strands of floss.
☆	702		226	green						

Each design was stitched on a 5" x 3" piece of Natural perforated paper (14 ct). Three strands of floss were used for Cross Stitch and 1 for Backstitch and Lazy Daisy Stitches, unless otherwise noted in the color key. See Working on Perforated Paper, page 143. They were made into spool ornaments.

(**Note:** We used $1^1/8$"h x $^7/8$" dia. wooden craft spools. If your spools are a different size, you may need to adjust the measurements of perforated paper and certain trims.)

For each ornament, trim stitched piece to measure approximately $2^7/8$" x $^7/8$". Wrap stitched piece around spool and glue in place. Glue a 3" length of $^1/16$"w ribbon around the top and bottom edges of stitched piece. Referring to photo, add yo-yos, tassels, or clothespins.

For each yo-yo, cut a $2^1/2$" dia. circle from fabric. Fold edge of fabric circle $^1/8$" to wrong side and baste as close to folded edge as possible; pull thread to gather tightly. Flatten circle, centering opening on one side. Thread a 9mm jingle bell onto a 12" length of $^1/16$"w ribbon. Thread needle with ribbon ends. Pull needle through one yo-yo (with gathered side against jingle bell), through spool, and through another yo-yo (with gathered side away from spool). Tie ribbon in a knot to secure. For hanger, tie ribbon ends in a knot. Tie a 6" length of $^1/8$"w ribbon in a bow and glue to top of yo-yo.

For each tassel, cut one 9" length of DMC 321 floss. Cut the remaining skein in 7" lengths; align the lengths. Knot 9" length of floss around the middle of 7" lengths. Fold 7" lengths in half; for hanger, knot ends of 9" length. Slide spool over tassel.

For each candle holder, glue a $1^3/4$" clothespin to the bottom of spool. Place a 3"h x $^1/4$" dia. candle in the center of the spool.

Designs by Deanna Hall West.

129

Delivering gifts to good little boys and girls, Santa makes his way across a fleecy sweatshirt. The jolly gent will journey into your heart and brighten your holidays for years to come.

MERRY SANTA (61w x 86h)

X	DMC	¼X	B'ST	ANC.	COLOR
•	blanc	◹	◿	2	white
✖	310		◿	403	black
✚	321	◢		9046	red
▲	353	◢		6	dk peach
■	413			401	dk grey
⬖	433			358	dk brown
◉	434			310	brown
✦	435			1046	lt brown
◇	437			362	vy lt brown
★	498	◢		1005	dk red
⊖	502			877	green
▽	503			876	lt green
✕	666			46	lt red
=	676			891	lt gold
✔	677			886	vy lt gold
2	680			901	dk gold
%	725	◢	◿	305	yellow
4	729			890	gold
○	754			1012	peach
$	760	◢		1022	pink
❖	762	◢		234	lt grey
∏	782			308	vy dk yellow
⬠	783			307	dk yellow
▰	815			43	vy dk red
✚	931			1034	dk blue
C	932	◢		1033	blue
✳	948			1011	lt peach
T	3072	◢		847	grey
+	3752			1032	lt blue
⊙	3799			236	vy dk grey
⦿	310				black French Knot

The design was stitched over a 14" x 16" piece of 8.5 mesh waste canvas on a khaki sweatshirt. Six strands of floss were used for Cross Stitch and 2 for Backstitch and French Knots. The design was centered horizontally 1½" from the bottom of the neckband. See Working on Waste Canvas, page 143.

Design by Pat Olson.
Needlework adaptation by Jane Chandler.

With our pretty poinsettia garlands, it's easy to turn these simple projects into holiday favorites. The cheery mug and bread cloth set will add a splash of color to your Christmas repasts.

Mug: The design was repeated 4 times on a 10¼" x 3½" piece of Vinyl-Weave® (14 ct). Three strands of floss were used for Cross Stitch and 1 for Backstitch. For placement, stitch the first design with the top edge 5 squares from the top edge of the vinyl and the left edge 14 squares from the left edge of the vinyl. It was inserted in a red mug. Hand wash mug to protect stitchery.

Bread Cover: The design, omitting the stripes, was repeated 4 times on one side of a white bread cover (14 ct). Three strands of floss were used for Cross Stitch and 2 for Backstitch. For placement, center the design horizontally with the bottom edge ½" from beginning of fringe.

To finish the corners of the bread cover, cut 3" squares out of each corner. Machine stitch ½" away from raw edges; fringe fabric to machine-stitched lines.

Design by Jane Chandler.

X	DMC	B'ST	COLOR
I	469		green
X	471		lt green
▷	666		lt red
✦	725		lt gold
	780	╲	dk gold

X	DMC	B'ST	COLOR
✦	783		gold
○	816		red
	902	╲	dk red
	936	╲	dk green

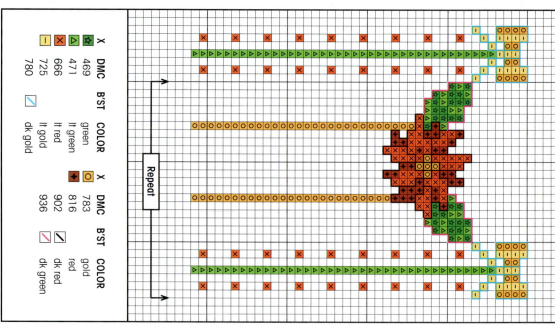

HO-HO-HO TOTE

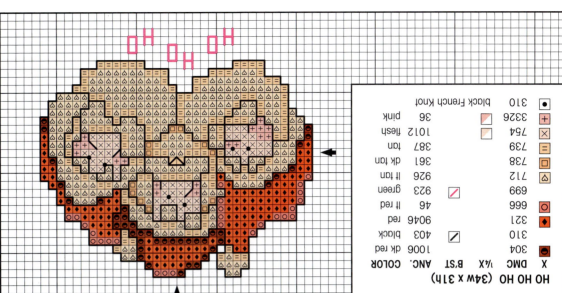

Design by Karen Wood.

The design was stitched on an Ivory Lil' Tote (14 ct). Three strands of floss were used for Cross Stitch and 1 for Backstitch and French Knots.

Ho Ho Ho — three Santas in a row add a jovial touch to this tiny tote. The fast-to-finish project makes a merry gift bag when packed with a small token of your affection.

HO HO HO (34w x 31h)

X	DMC	¼X	B'ST	ANC.	COLOR
	304			1006	dk red
✓	310		✓	403	black
◆	321			9046	red
○	666			46	lt red
	699		✓	923	green
△	712			926	lt tan
□	738			361	dk tan
▬	739			387	tan
✕	754			1012	flesh
+	3326			36	pink
●	310				black French Knot

YULETIDE SOCKS

Family and friends will kick up their heels when you give them these Yuletide socks! The myriad of quick-to-stitch motifs makes it easy and inexpensive to present a pair to everyone on your Christmas list.

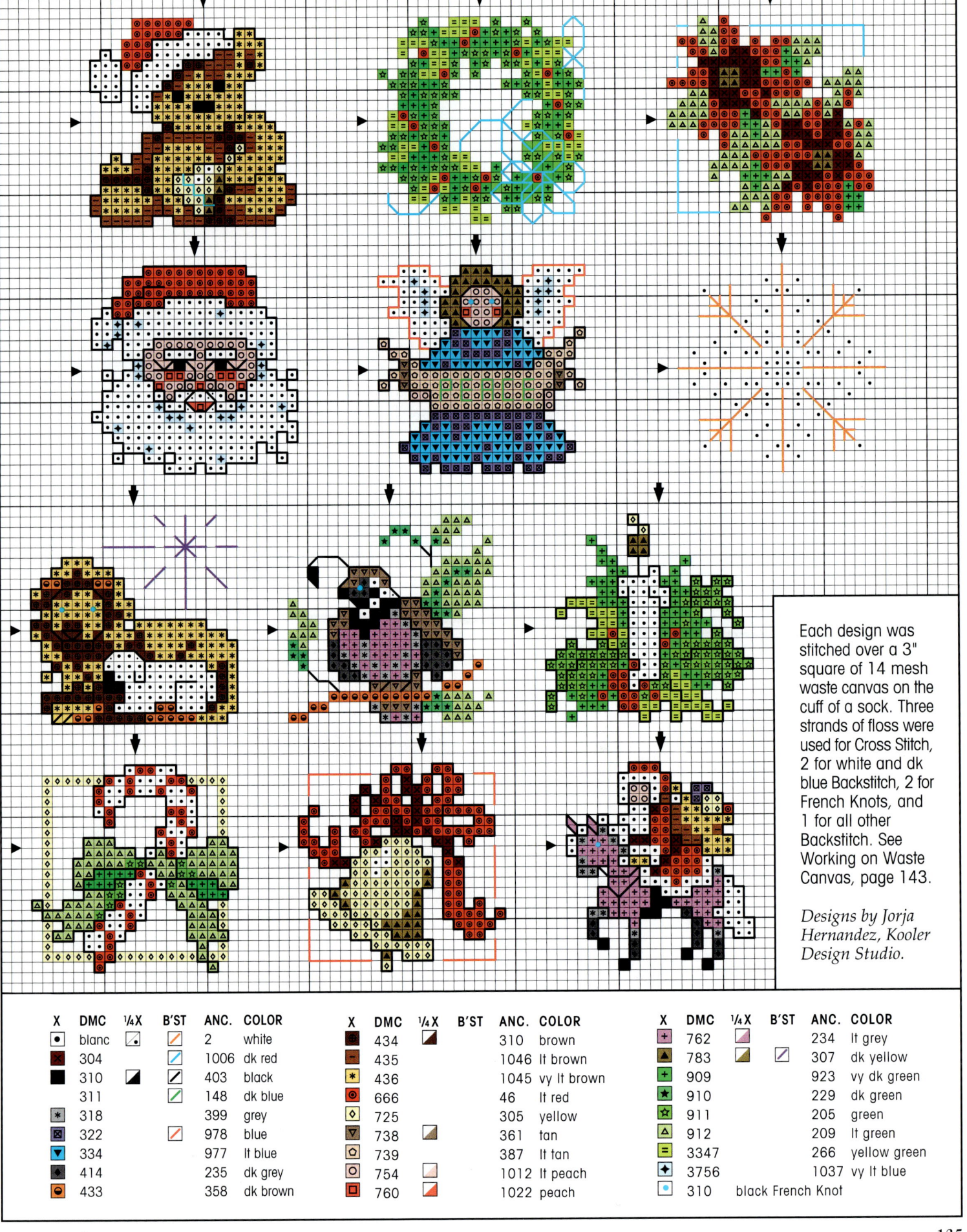

Each design was stitched over a 3" square of 14 mesh waste canvas on the cuff of a sock. Three strands of floss were used for Cross Stitch, 2 for white and dk blue Backstitch, 2 for French Knots, and 1 for all other Backstitch. See Working on Waste Canvas, page 143.

Designs by Jorja Hernandez, Kooler Design Studio.

X	DMC	¼X	B'ST	ANC.	COLOR
●	blanc			2	white
	304			1006	dk red
■	310			403	black
	311			148	dk blue
*	318			399	grey
	322			978	blue
▼	334			977	lt blue
	414			235	dk grey
	433			358	dk brown

X	DMC	¼X	B'ST	ANC.	COLOR
	434			310	brown
	435			1046	lt brown
*	436			1045	vy lt brown
◉	666			46	lt red
◇	725			305	yellow
▽	738			361	tan
	739			387	lt tan
○	754			1012	lt peach
□	760			1022	peach

X	DMC	¼X	B'ST	ANC.	COLOR
+	762			234	lt grey
▲	783			307	dk yellow
+	909			923	vy dk green
★	910			229	dk green
☆	911			205	green
△	912			209	lt green
=	3347			266	yellow green
✦	3756			1037	vy lt blue
●	310				black French Knot

135

Welcome holiday guests in from the cold with our merry mugs filled with hot drinks or tasty treats. Each is trimmed with festive motifs, glad tidings, and cheery borders.

MERRY MUGS

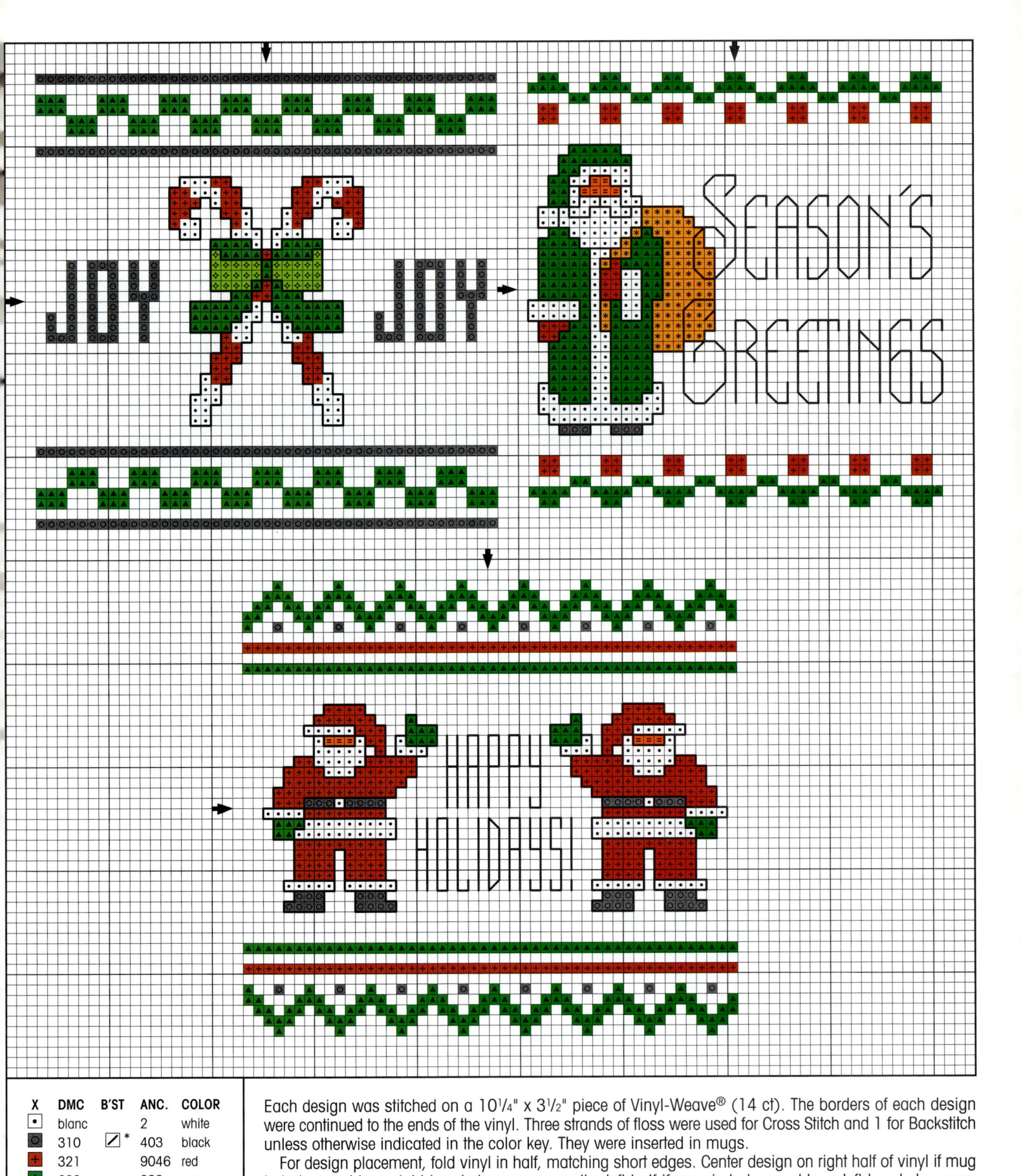

X	DMC	B'ST	ANC.	COLOR
·	blanc		2	white
◉	310	⁄ *	403	black
+	321		9046	red
▲	699		923	green
✧	702		226	lt green
*	783		307	gold
=	948		1011	peach

* Use 2 strands of floss for words.

Each design was stitched on a 10¼" x 3½" piece of Vinyl-Weave® (14 ct). The borders of each design were continued to the ends of the vinyl. Three strands of floss were used for Cross Stitch and 1 for Backstitch unless otherwise indicated in the color key. They were inserted in mugs.

For design placement, fold vinyl in half, matching short edges. Center design on right half of vinyl if mug is to be used by a right-handed person or on the left half if mug is to be used by a left-handed person. Hand wash mug to protect stitchery.

Designs by Deborah Lambein.

137

Homespun hearts and checkered borders give these bread cloths a warm country look. They feature two of our favorite holiday symbols — a snowman and gingerbread men.

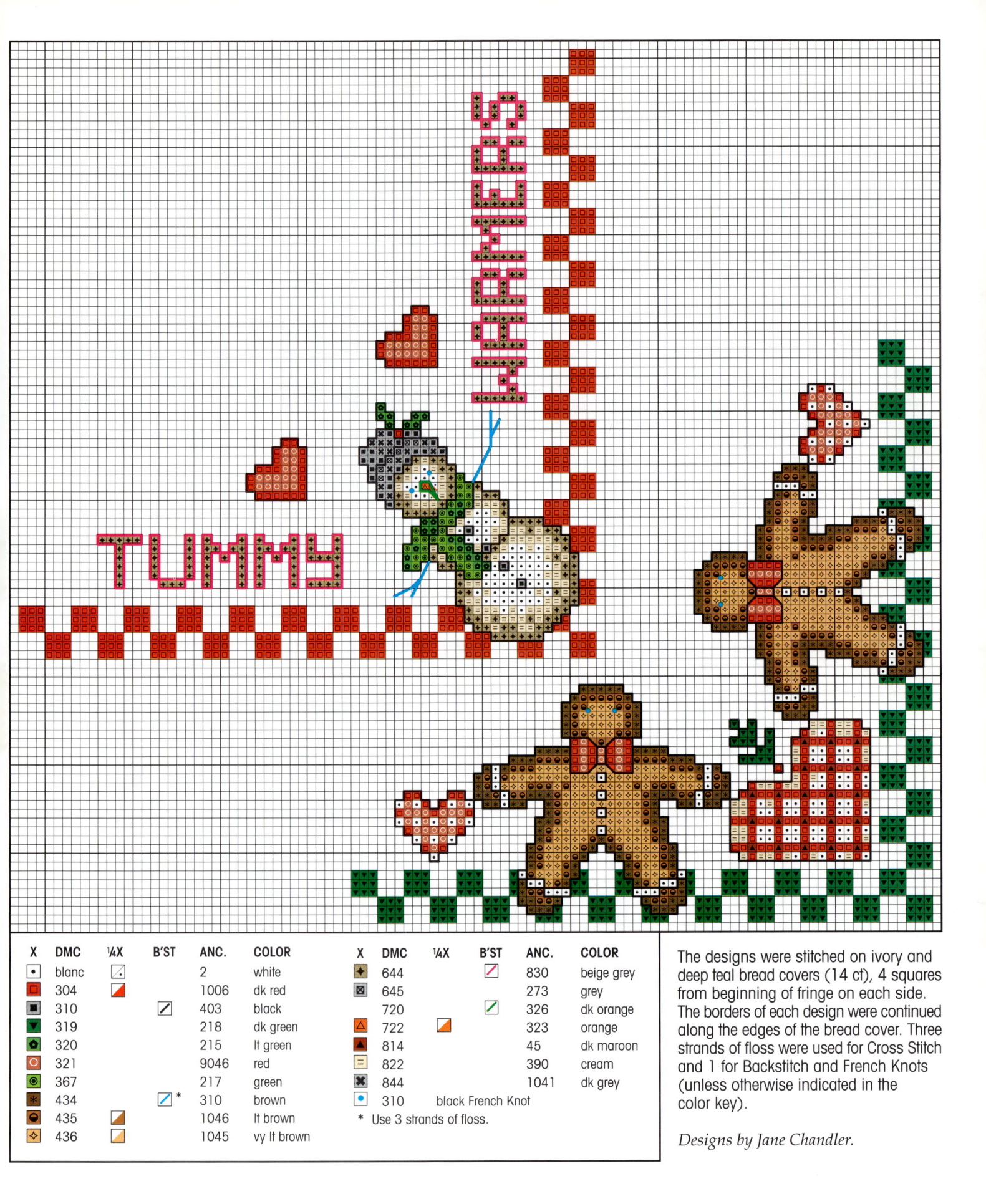

X	DMC	¼X	B'ST	ANC.	COLOR		X	DMC	¼X	B'ST	ANC.	COLOR
•	blanc			2	white			644			830	beige grey
□	304			1006	dk red			645			273	grey
■	310			403	black			720			326	dk orange
▼	319			218	dk green			722			323	orange
⬠	320			215	lt green			814			45	dk maroon
○	321			9046	red			822			390	cream
◉	367			217	green			844			1041	dk grey
✳	434			310	brown *			310				black French Knot
●	435			1046	lt brown							
✧	436			1045	vy lt brown							

* Use 3 strands of floss.

The designs were stitched on ivory and deep teal bread covers (14 ct), 4 squares from beginning of fringe on each side. The borders of each design were continued along the edges of the bread cover. Three strands of floss were used for Cross Stitch and 1 for Backstitch and French Knots (unless otherwise indicated in the color key).

Designs by Jane Chandler.

ADORABLE ACCENTS

Create an array of adorable accents for the holidays with these miniature motifs. We stitched two of them on cheery towels and fashioned one into a keepsake ornament. You'll find dozens of uses for these little Christmas designs!

The **Mouse** and **Wreath** designs were each stitched on the 14 ct border of a red plaid towel. Three strands of floss were used for Cross Stitch and 1 for Backstitch and French Knots.

The **Candy Cane** design was stitched on a 6" square of Natural Aida (14 ct). Three strands of floss were used for Cross Stitch and 1 for Backstitch. It was inserted in a purchased frame (3½" dia. opening).

Designs by Karen Wood.

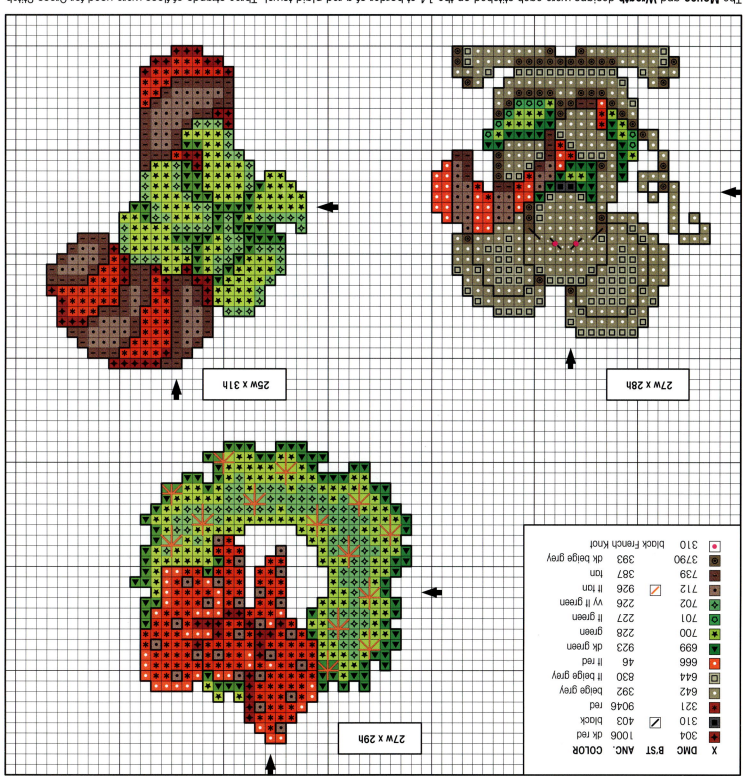

27w x 29h

25w x 31h

27w x 28h

X	DMC	ANC.	B'ST	COLOR
	304	1006		dk red
	310	403	⟋	black
	321	9046		red
	642	392		beige grey
	644	830		lt beige grey
	666	46		lt red
	699	923		dk green
	700	228		green
	701	227		lt green
	702	226		vy lt green
	712	926	⟋	lt tan
	739	387		tan
	3790	393		dk beige grey
	310			black French Knot

GENERAL INSTRUCTIONS
WORKING WITH CHARTS

How to Read Charts: Each of the designs is shown in chart form. Each colored square on the chart represents one Cross Stitch or one Half Cross Stitch. Each colored triangle on the chart represents one One-Quarter Stitch or one Three-Quarter Stitch. Black or colored dots represent French Knots. Black or colored ovals represent Lazy Daisy Stitches. The straight lines on the chart indicate Backstitch. When a French Knot, Lazy Daisy Stitch, or Backstitch covers a square, the symbol is omitted or a reduced symbol is shown.

Each chart is accompanied by a color key. This key indicates the color of floss to use for each stitch on the chart. The headings on the color key are for Cross Stitch (X), One-Quarter Stitch (¹/₄X), Three-Quarter Stitch (³/₄X), Half Cross Stitch (¹/₂X), Backstitch (B'ST), DMC color number (DMC), Anchor color number (ANC) or J. & P. Coats color number (JPC), and color name (COLOR). Color key columns should be read vertically and horizontally to determine type of stitch and floss color.

How to Determine Finished Size: The finished size of your design will depend on the thread count per inch of the fabric being used. To determine the finished size of the design on different fabrics, divide the number of squares (stitches) in the width of the charted design by the thread count of the fabric. For example, a charted design with a width of 80 squares worked on 14 count Aida will yield a design 5³/₄" wide. Repeat for the number of squares (stitches) in the height of the charted design. (**Note:** To work over two fabric threads, divide the number of squares by one-half the thread count.) Then add the amount of background you want plus a generous amount for finishing.

Where to Start: The horizontal and vertical centers of the charted design are shown by arrows. You may start at any point on the charted design, but be sure the design will be centered on the fabric. Locate the center of the fabric by folding in half, top to bottom and again left to right. On the charted design, count the number of squares from the center of the chart to the determined starting point, then from the fabric's center, count out the same number of fabric threads.

STITCH DIAGRAMS

Counted Cross Stitch (X): For horizontal rows, work stitches in two journeys (**Fig. 1**). For vertical rows, complete each stitch as shown (**Fig. 2**). When working over two fabric threads, work Cross Stitch as shown in **Fig. 3**. When the chart shows a Backstitch crossing a colored square (**Fig. 4**), a Cross Stitch should be worked first; then the Backstitch (**Fig. 9 or 10**) should be worked on top of the Cross Stitch.

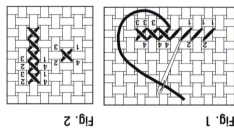

Fig. 1   Fig. 2

Fig. 3   Fig. 4

Quarter Stitch (¹/₄X and ³/₄X): Come up at 1 (**Fig. 5**); then split fabric thread to go down at 2 to complete a One-Quarter Stitch. When stitches 1-4 are worked in the same color, the resulting stitch is called a Three-Quarter Stitch (³/₄X). **Fig. 6** shows the technique for Quarter Stitches when working over 2 fabric threads.

Fig. 5   Fig. 6

Half Cross Stitch (¹/₂X): This stitch is one journey of the Cross Stitch and is worked from lower left to upper right as shown in **Fig. 7**. When working over two fabric threads, work Half Cross Stitch as shown in **Fig. 8**.

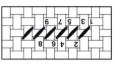

Fig. 7   Fig. 8

Backstitch (B'ST): For outline detail, Backstitch should be worked after the design has been completed (**Fig. 9**). When working over two fabric threads, work Backstitch as shown in **Fig. 10**.

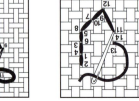

Fig. 9   Fig. 10

French Knot: Bring needle up at 1. Wrap floss once around needle and insert needle at 2, holding end of floss with non-stitching fingers (**Fig. 11**). Tighten knot; then pull needle through fabric, holding floss until it must be released. For larger knot, use more strands; wrap only once.

Fig. 11

Lazy Daisy Stitch: Bring needle up at 1 and make a loop. Go down at 1 and come up at 2 to anchor loop, keeping floss below point of needle (**Fig. 12**). Pull needle through and go down at 2, completing stitch. (**Note:** To support stitches, it may be helpful to go down in edge of next fabric thread when anchoring loop.)

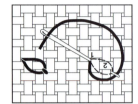

Fig. 12

STITCHING TIPS

Working over Two Fabric Threads: Use the sewing method instead of the stab sewing method when working over two fabric threads. To use the sewing method, keep your stitching hand on the right side of the fabric (instead of stabbing the fabric with the needle and taking your stitching hand to the back of the fabric to pick up the needle). With the sewing method, you take the needle down and up with one stroke instead of two. To add support to stitches, it is important that the first Cross Stitch is placed on the fabric beginning and ending where a vertical fabric thread crosses over a horizontal fabric thread (Fig. 13). When the first stitch is in the correct position, the entire design will be placed properly, with vertical fabric threads supporting each stitch.

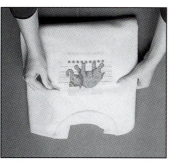

Fig. 13

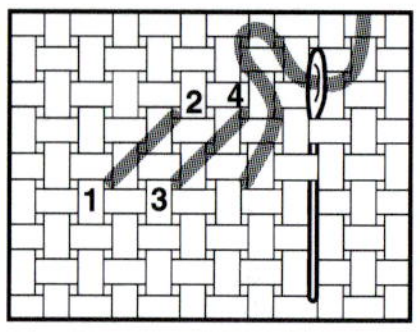

Working on Waste Canvas: Waste canvas (also known as tear-away cloth or waste cloth) is a special canvas that provides an evenweave grid for placing stitches on fabric. After the design is worked over the canvas, the canvas threads are removed, leaving the design on the fabric. Most canvas has blue parallel threads every fifth square to aid in counting and in placing the canvas straight on the fabric. The blue threads may be placed horizontally or vertically. The canvas is available in several mesh sizes. Use lightweight, nonfusible interfacing on wrong side of fabric to give a firmer stitching base. We recommend a screw-type hoop that is large enough to encircle the entire design. Use a #24 tapestry needle for tightly knit fabric. Use a sharp embroidery needle for tightly knit or tightly woven fabric. To ensure smoother stitches, separate floss strands and realign them before threading the needle.

Step 1. Cut waste canvas 2" larger than design size on all sides. Cut interfacing same size as canvas. To prevent raw edges of canvas from marring fabric, cover edges of canvas with masking tape.

Step 2. Find desired placement for design; mark center of design on garment with a pin.

Step 3. Match center of canvas to pin. Use the blue threads in canvas to place canvas straight on garment; pin canvas to garment. To prevent canvas from slipping, especially on large designs, baste securely around edge of canvas through all three thicknesses. Then baste from corner to corner and from side to side as shown in Fig. 14.

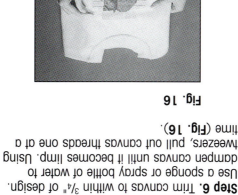

Fig. 14

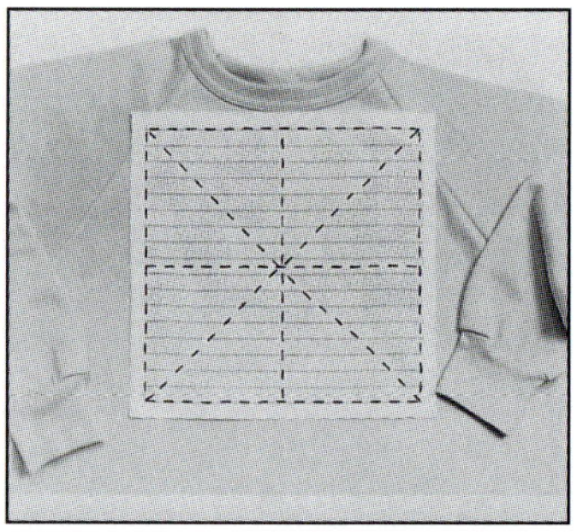

Step 4. Place garment in hoop. The hoop helps keep the area not being stitched out of the way. Roll excess fabric, including back of garment, over top edge of hoop and pin in place (Fig. 15).

Fig. 15

Step 5. Work design following Stitch Diagrams.

Step 6. Trim canvas to within 3/4" of design. Use a sponge or spray bottle of water to dampen canvas until it becomes limp. Using tweezers, pull out canvas threads one at a time (Fig. 16).

Fig. 16

Step 7. Trim interfacing close to design.

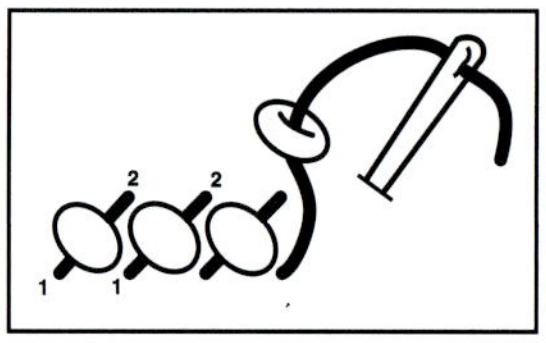

FINISHING TECHNIQUES

PHOTO FRAME FINISHING
Continued from page 12.

To finish frame, refer to chart and color key to cut along outside and inside cutting lines. Using 2 strands of ecru embroidery floss, work Blanket Stitch around outside edge of frame.

For frame backing, cut one piece of perforated paper 1/4" larger on all sides than desired photo measurement. Center backing on wrong side of photo frame and glue side and bottom edges in place.

BE MINE PILLOW FINISHING
Continued from page 13.

Note: Use a 1/2" seam allowance for all seams.

Centering design, trim stitched piece to measure 7 1/2" x 6". Cut a piece of fabric the same size as stitched piece for backing.

For cording, cut one 2" x 30" bias strip of fabric. Center 30" length of 1/4" dia. cord on wrong side of bias strip, matching long edges; fold strip over cord. Using zipper foot, baste along length of strip close to cord, trim seam allowances to 1/2". Matching raw edges and beginning at bottom edge, pin cording to right side of stitched piece, making a 3/8" clip in seam

Working on Perforated Paper: Perforated paper has a right side and a wrong side. The right side is smoother and stitching should be done on this side. To find the center, do not fold the paper; use a ruler and mark lightly with a pencil, or count holes. Perforated paper will tear if handled roughly; therefore, hold paper flat while stitching and do not use a hoop. Begin and end stitching by running floss under several stitches on the back; never use knots. Use the stab method when stitching. Carry floss across back as little as possible. Thread pulled too tightly may tear the paper. Keep stitching tension consistent.

Attaching Beads: Refer to chart for bead placement and sew bead in place using 1 strand of embroidery floss and a fine needle that will pass through the bead. Bring needle up through hole, run needle down through hole then up through hole of next bead. Secure floss on back as shown in Fig. 17 making a Half Cross Stitch to secure floss or move to next bead.

Fig. 17

allowances of cording at each corner. Ends of cording should overlap approx. 2"; pin overlapping end out of the way. Starting 1 1/2" from beginning of cording and ending 3" from overlapping end, sew cording to stitched piece. On overlapping end of cording, remove 2" of basting; fold end of fabric back and trim cord so it meets beginning end of fabric. Fold end of fabric under 1/2"; wrap fabric over beginning end of cording. Finish sewing cording to stitched piece.

For ruffle, press short ends of a 3" x 75" piece of flat lace 1/2" to wrong side. Gather lace to fit stitched piece. Matching raw edges and beginning at bottom edge, pin ruffle to right side of stitched piece, overlapping short ends 1/4"; sew ruffle to stitched piece.

Matching right sides and leaving an opening for turning, sew stitched piece and backing fabric together. Trim corners diagonally. Turn pillow right side out. Stuff pillow with polyester fiberfill and sew final closure by hand.

For bow, cut seven 18" lengths of assorted widths and colors of ribbon. Align ends and tie in a bow. Refer to photo and thread charms on ribbon ends; knot to secure. Tack bow to pillow.

APPLE PILLOW FINISHING

Continued from page 54.

Note: Use a 1/2" seam allowance for all seams.

Centering design, trim stitched piece to desired size. Cut a piece of fabric the same size as the stitched piece for backing.

For cording, cut a bias strip of fabric 2" wide and the outer dimension of the pillow top plus 2". (**Note:** This strip may be pieced if necessary.) Center 1/4" dia. cord on wrong side of bias strip, matching long edges; fold strip over cord. Using zipper foot, baste along length of strip close to cord; trim seam allowances to 1/2".

Matching raw edges and beginning at bottom edge, pin cording to right side of stitched piece, making a 3/8" clip in seam allowances of cording at each corner. Ends of cording should overlap approx. 2"; pin overlapping end out of the way. Starting 1 1/2" from beginning of cording and ending 3" from overlapping end, sew cording to stitched piece. On overlapping end of cording, remove 2" of basting; fold end of fabric back and trim cord so it meets beginning end of cord. Fold end of fabric under 1/2"; wrap fabric over beginning end of cording. Finish sewing cording to stitched piece.

For ruffle, cut a strip of fabric twice the desired finished width plus 1" for seam allowances and twice the outer dimension of the stitched piece. (**Note:** This strip may be pieced if necessary.) Press short ends of ruffle 1/2" to wrong side. Gather ruffle to fit stitched piece. Matching raw edges and beginning at bottom edge, pin ruffle to right side of stitched piece, overlapping short ends 1/4"; sew ruffle to stitched piece.

Matching right sides and leaving an opening for turning, sew stitched piece and backing fabric together. Trim corners diagonally. Turn pillow right side out. Stuff pillow with polyester fiberfill and sew final closure by hand.

JAR LID FINISHING

Mason jar puff-up kits may be purchased for both regular and wide-mouth jar lids; mounting instructions are included in kit. If a kit is not available, a padded mounting board can be made. Using flat piece of lid for pattern, cut a circle from adhesive mounting board. Using opening of screw ring for pattern, cut a circle of batting. Center batting on adhesive side of board; press into place. Center stitched piece on board and press adhesive onto edges of board. Trim edges close to board. Glue board inside screw ring.

STIFFENED ITEM FINISHING

Cut a piece of cotton fabric for backing same size as stitched piece. Apply fabric stiffener to back of stitched piece. Matching wrong sides, place stitched piece on backing fabric; allow to dry. Apply stiffener to back of item; allow to dry. Trim to 1/2" square around edges of design. To prevent fraying, apply a small amount of stiffener to edges of design; allow to dry.